Dear Fathers of the Fatherless Children

Charlena E. Jackson, B.S., M.S., M.H.A

Cover design by Annabelle Pullen Instagram username (@artofannabellepullen) artofannabellepullen@gmail.com

Printed in the United States of America
1st edition, October, 2019
ISBN 978-1-7340704-1-5

BOOKS BY CHARLENA E. JACKSON, B.S., M.S., M.H.A

To my daddy, Alexander Jackson, with love. Daddy, you are such an amazing father! Thank you for always being in my life. Your presence made me the woman who I am today! You always believed in me, and I will always and forever be grateful! People always say, "You act just like your Daddy." I tell them, "I sure do, and I wouldn't have it any other way!"

To my brother, Miles Jackson. You are a wonderful father! You are a loving, patient, and understanding father. My nieces and nephew are blessed!

To Grandpa, Chris Crenshaw, you are the best Grandpa in the universe. You are always there and never missed an event. Thank you for always being at every Grandparents Day, every game, and graduation, you never missed a milestone! We are so grateful for your presence and love. We love you dearly!

To all of the fathers in the world who are in their children's lives, you all are the foundation in your son's and daughter's lives. Your presence makes a huge difference. A father's love cannot be replaced. Fathers, you all are such a blessing!

~ Dedicated to my granddaddy Tom Miles 1914-2003 ~

Contents

Introduction

The choices we make in life can make or break us. However, some people make choices out of selfish reasons; not knowing their actions at the present time will have repercussions in the future. We are told not to worry about tomorrow; for tomorrow is not promised. That could be very well true. However, what if tomorrow *is* promised; how would you reexamine yesterday? What would you do differently today? How would you prepare for tomorrow?

We are told to live for today, however, the question is—how many people live for "today?" If you are living for "today" at the end of the day, could you say you took care of all of your responsibilities? Each day has a purpose; each day creates a memory, and each day should be precious.

Ask yourself—did you put your best foot forward? Or did you point fingers at everyone else instead of focusing on what you need to improve? The important question is: at the end of each day are you satisfied with the decisions you've made?

Dear Fathers of the Fatherless Children:

Do you know your sons and daughters are AMAZING? They are full of life and they are truly a blessing. Your sons and daughters need you in their lives. How is it possible that at the beginning of the day when you open your eyes, your children are not on your priority list? Fathers of the fatherless children, your sons and daughters crave your presence and your support. They want you in their lives more than you will ever know. There isn't such a thing as a part-time father; your children shouldn't be treated as toys that you can throw in the closet when you are tired or when the going gets rough. Your sons and daughters are human; they should feel loved and nothing less at all times. You say you love your children, but actions speak louder than words; stand up and be a father to your sons and daughters.

Fathers of the fatherless children, open your eyes and know your presence is very critical. Be your son's hero and let him know he can conquer the world. Be your daughter's first knight in shining armor. Be a part of your son's and daughter's success instead of their pain.

1

Family Foundation and Structure

The most valuable asset in your life should be your family. Each family has its ups and downs; however, at the end of the day, family will be there for each other. Family doesn't consist of the blood that is running through your veins. Family is the people who have been there for you; through thick and thin, happy and challenging times; they are the ones who've always believed in you, no matter how deep you've fallen or how high you've jumped.

Family is the foundation of a powerful force; such as guidance, building character, morality, respect, honesty, handling responsibilities, making memories and teaches you the fundamentals of life.

Family structure is a source of empowerment; it develops great strength and it is your turbo-charged to recovery from the lessons that didn't work in your favor. When times are difficult, family helps you work through your conflict. They are supportive when you feel helpless and hopeless; they bring forth determination when you are at your lowest point.

Family comes together to help you remember your purpose and why you started. Having support from your family is critical; not only does it show they care, but they know you are only human. They give you the strength to dive deep, come up for air, step back, recharge, rest, and reconnect.

I had the best of both worlds. I was raised by my mother and her parents, and my daddy and his parents, my daddy's grandmother and I had another grandmother who helped raised me as well. Therefore, I had four grandmothers, two grandfathers, my parents, my aunts, uncles, and older cousins who valued family structure and laid down the foundation.

My mother's mom is very strict, but as I got older, I understood why. My mother's father was the foundation in my grandparent's household. He taught my siblings and me that we could do anything if we put our minds to it. My granddaddy was a hard worker, and he led by example.

My daddy's mother was a ball of fire and very bold; she would set you straight in a minute. However, she had a good heart as well. She taught us that it is okay to be bold, speak your mind, and stand for what you believe in. My daddy's dad taught us that time moves at a steady pace and it doesn't wait on anyone. He was good at getting who and what he wanted. My daddy's grandma (who was my great-grandma), we called her Big Momma. She took care of the neighbors, and she was highly respected. She taught us that we don't always have to have the last word. She preached about keeping our mouths shut (when needed), and to keep our eyes and ears open at all times.

My mother is a go-getter. She was a wife and mother. As a little girl; I saw my mother go through a lot—she had her ups and downs, but it wasn't anything she didn't conquer. My mother's fundamentals from her upbringing set boundaries and family structure in our household.

My daddy is very intelligent. There is no such thing as reading between the lines when it comes to him; trust me when I say he will let you know what he wants you to know. He is very blunt and he gets straight to the point. He doesn't sugar coat what he says. He will let you know how it is and how it is going to be – without hesitation. When it comes to his girls, he is very sensitive and humble with his words. My daddy laid the foundation and structure in our household.

When it comes to my aunts, uncles, and older cousins in my family, they played a valuable role as well. My aunts, uncles, and cousin on my mother's side were very humble and understanding; they were sensitive and gentle when it came to family. Some of my cousins were very competitive when education was involved. My mother's side was highly educated and disciplined.

My aunts, uncles, and older cousins on my daddy's side were totally different. Unlike my mother's side, they were street- and book-smart. My daddy's side was straightforward and they were always encouraging. There wasn't such a thing as competition. They wanted us to have a better life than they did; they were our coaches, biggest fans of never giving up, and they made sure we remembered to always make each day count as if it was our last.

Family structure doesn't always require for the parents to reside in the same household; sometimes that isn't always possible. Family structure is defined by what an individual (mother, father, grandparents, extended relatives, and friends) has instilled in someone out of fulfillment, from loving, caring, and growing in wisdom.

Nowadays, there is a high percentage of mothers who are laying down the foundation of the home and family structure. Give or take the single mother's parents (mother/father) might be involved; however, when it is all said and done, most of the time the mother is carrying the load alone. It doesn't have to be that way. Just because the mother and father have their differences; the child shouldn't suffer or be robbed of guidance and family structure from both their mother and father.

Our sons and daughters are born as roses without thorns; However, as they grow, thorns appear as they become observers. They begin to transition their thoughts, not only by what they see but also by what they hear. As time passes, our children are painting a picture that represents their present reality and development of their future. These are stages where the side effects take place, which causes emotional struggles when obstacles occur, as conflicted issues are difficult to resolve.

When our sons and daughters are young, as parents, we are writing the chapters in their lives. As they grow and become wiser, we are responsible for our actions and for the words that effortlessly flow from our mouths.

Dysfunctional behaviors become patterns as they grow, like flesh-eating bacteria, when there isn't structure in our children's lives. Our sons and daughters begin to fight an internal war because they are misguided by our actions and words. I have noticed that this appears when the mother and father do not get along with each other. The children are caught in the middle of a battle that they think is their fault or a battle that is not theirs to fight.

We fail to realize that as parents we put our children in an uncomfortable state of mind. We overlook the symptoms of their silent anger and the wear and tear of our fragile children. What makes matters worse, our sons and daughters begin to choose sides and begin to judge the parent they feel is reflecting the most pain. Which is so unfair to our children.

Instead of parents working through their conflicts, our sons and daughters, who were born without thorns, now have the thorns of misery, manipulation, distance, burdens, shortcomings, and abandonment. Our children are filled with a world of distractions; which causes them to make difficult decisions, to stray off-track and become vulnerable to life's challenges.

Family structure is important to our children. It contains the building blocks that form the foundation of love and stability. In order for our sons and daughters to feel love and know what love is, requires time. We must make time for our children. Time is very precious because time doesn't wait for anyone. Therefore, we must make the best of the time we are given. As we spend time and engage in our son's and daughter's lives, we are showing them what love is. That way, they will feel and know that they are loved.

Unconditional time and love build our son's and daughter's character. Time and love inspire our children to dream; this gives them the opportunity to make their dreams a reality. Time and love open our children's eyes to reflect on their core values in life; this produces great leadership, perseverance, and strength.

If a household doesn't have family structure, turmoil will be created in the minds and hearts of our children. Our sons and daughters will have the mindset that they would rather give up than fail. Doubt will be their only way out if they don't have a little faith. They will be more willing to make poor judgments because they feel as though they do not have anything to lose. They are not thinking about the consequences that will unfold;

therefore, they take fearful chances. Their character will be tainted because they have formed traits from the world which is "raising them."

Family structure is the foundation of our household. If we neglect to form a tight bond of family structure with our sons and daughters the world will deal them a bitter cutthroat hand. The odds will never be in our children's favor. Our precious sons and daughters will always be at war with the world and themselves. The world will steal their souls to the point where they will be searching for their identity. Our sons and daughters will be searching for a place to fit in; in this world, we call home.

We as their parents must give our children a chance, and that chance starts with letting our sons and daughters know we love and support them.

I am a firm believer that learning begins at home. Before our children get a taste of this cold, cruel, bitter-sweet world we have the ability to teach our sons and daughters that they are courageous in so many ways, they are one-of-a-kind; and it is okay to be different. We must teach our children to accept the skin they are in, and it is okay to be a shade lighter or darker. We must love on our children; hug our children and let them know they are perfect just the way they are.

Family structure consists of letting our sons and daughters live and learn. When they are young, it is our duty to let them know that failure isn't the end; however, it is the beginning of knowing what will and will not work for them. That way, as they grow and become wiser, they will not be afraid to fail; they will have a positive attitude and humbly move forward to something new.

Honesty is a form of family structure as well because we do not want to form a pattern of lying to our children to make them feel good. Truth be told, the world is filled with compulsive liars, who are very blunt and filled with so much rudeness. We have to teach our sons and daughters that criticism isn't a bad thing. I have noticed that nowadays, there are a lot of children who don't take criticism well. Criticism shuts them down and dampens their personality to an "I don't give a care" kind of child. It is our responsibility to instill in our sons and daughters to take what they can use from criticism to make them a better person in life and to throw away what is not needed.

Family structure consists of building confidence in our sons and daughters, starting from when they are young. Therefore, when their foundation begins to shake, they will know how to keep what serves them and leave what doesn't behind as they hit the ground running. Every now and then, confidence is complemented by rejection. Rejection might put a damper on their spirits for a moment, but the confidence they gain from not allowing rejection to rip them apart comes from having a strong family structure. With that being said, they will understand that rejection is a part of life; and life is filled with rejections and accomplishments. It is how they handle both that will help them travel down the road we call life.

Family structure is our children's support system. It builds a healthy home for our children. Not only does it build a healthy home, but it also builds a healthier society. Our sons and daughters will know that love, discipline, and taking responsibility starts first at home. As they step out in the world, they will have a clear understanding; society does not have the ability to make or break them. They will have the concept that a strong-willed and confident mind will take them further than the opinions of what others have to offer. Our sons and daughters will contribute to help form a healthier society because their support system started at home.

Patience and understanding are part of family structure. As parents, we must not leave any wounds open; we must fill all voids by listening, being patient, and understanding our children's needs. Being willing to give our children our undivided attention counts more than we could ever imagine.

Leading by example is an important part of family structure as well. We teach our sons and daughters by our example of hard work. As they live and learn by observing our mistakes and struggles first-hand, they will have a sense of reality that nothing comes easy; everything worth having is earned; most definitely, not given. As they look up to us as parents, our sons and daughters will have a keen insight that there's no such thing as a short cut in life. If we don't lead by example, they will have the mentality of always starting over without completing anything; and we do not want that for our children.

We are our son's and daughter's role models, guides, coaches, and number one fans! However, sadly, the word "parents" is not a common word nowadays. The plural "S" has cowardly taken itself off the word; and prefers to be called "selfish, slacker, and sorry dead-beat Dad."

Fathers of the fatherless sons and daughters, you need to get your act together. There are too many fathers who are ripping and running the street who do not provide for their children or lead by example. There are too many fathers who do not have a care in the world about how their sons and daughters are doing. There are too many fathers of the fatherless children who make up one too many excuses about why they can't provide, care, or make time for their sons and daughters. There are too many fathers who are too selfish to realize that their children need them.

Fathers of the fatherless children, your presence is needed in your precious son's and daughter's life. Whether you care to know it or not, you are a huge part of your son's and daughter's foundation. If you were in their life, believe it or not, their confidence would be to the moon and back. Your support system would mean the entire universe to them. However, your definition of "family structure" is being a father that is selfish, a slacker, "sperm donor," and a self-centered person because you're only looking out for yourself.

Note to all of the fathers of the fatherless sons and daughters, there is no way you can love yourself without taking care of your responsibilities. Sadly, your unknown presence is your son's and daughter's first rejection in life.

2

Identity Crisis

More than ever, our sons and daughters are suffering internally because they do not know who they are as a person. They question their worthiness of being loved and accepted. Silently, our children are fighting many burdens that we will never know; tears that are hidden; strength that they never gained; courage that doesn't exist; pain that is covered up, and breakdowns that are unseen by the naked eye.

At full speed, without brakes, our son's and daughter's lives are crumbling because they are carrying heavy loads, trying to figure out where they fit in this world. This is a huge problem because our sons and daughters are trying to fix a problem that they do not know how to solve. They do not know where to start. They search high, low, inside, outside, and sideways, not knowing the answers come from their roots (their parents).

Our son's and daughter's identities are the foundation of who they are as a person. Their identity is a part of their character that develops as they age and grow into young men and women, and follows them as they enter the world as mature men and women.

Yet, as they are grown men and women, our children's identity has been stolen because of abandonment and neglect. They try to make do with what they were given, but the question is—is it enough? Is it fair that they can only identify with half of their roots, their DNA? Using a swab to send their DNA into a "DNA bank" isn't going to give them clarity about what they are missing from their lives on a day-to-day basis.

Face-to-face, hands-on and verbal communication are the deep roots that need to be exposed on the surface. The surface is their parents; both mother and father. However, in our son's and daughter's household nowadays, the only roots they have is from what they hear and see from their mother. Fathers of the fatherless children—where are you? Expose your roots so that your children will not have to suffer from identity crises because of your absences and lack of judgment.

There are several identity crises our sons and daughters suffer from on a daily basis. They struggle, trying to understand why they weren't good enough for their father to give them a chance at love. Although they know their mother's love is never-ending, there is a void. Where is my father? Where is his love? Why couldn't I have been given a chance for him to love me? And me to love him?

Father of the fatherless children, because of your absences, your children's lack of identity has crushed their self-esteem and confidence. This lack of identity has stomped all over their ability to trust. Their father is the reason why they aren't able to trust anyone due to his neglect without cause.

Fathers of the fatherless sons and daughters, that void will never close because it's something your children will always want to know the answer to. Regardless of how old your children are—they will always be your children. If they contact you when they are grown and/or have children of their own, they will ask you why didn't you love them or allow them to love you in return? Man up and give them an answer. Sadly, for your children, but a known fact, you took the easy way out. The responsibilities of raising your children and providing financial assistance are no longer required. Answer their questions—they deserve to know the truth. You owe them that much.

Also, in our society today, we have what I call the "revolving door" fathers that come in and out of their children's lives, and who are known as the part-time fathers of the fatherless sons and daughters. They aren't any better than the fathers who simply disappeared. Part-time fathers of the fatherless children, it is beyond shameful that you have to "pencil" your child into your schedule once every blue moon. Sad, but inevitable, you play the victim when your children don't want to be bothered. They are tired of being a part of the central axis in your "revolving doors" as the turning of confusion is never-ending. Your sons and daughters are tired of their spirits being lifted by your false lies. Once again, over and over repeatedly, you disappoint and drop them at any giving moment without considering their feelings. Little do you know, they become lost and buried in their emotional identity.

Your children's emotional identity is a huge part of their mental capacity. It is their foremost feeling – such as feeling out of place, feeling unwanted, feeling of never being good enough, feelings about what have they've done wrong—as they plead to you, "Give me another chance, I'll try to fix it." Fathers of the fatherless children, your revolving doors mold your children's emotional identity for life.

Emotional identity is a major component of analyzing one's thoughts that leads to overthinking. It forms patterns in the brain that make your children feel a sense of loss, such as loss of control with one's self, to the point where your children start to think of hurting themselves, due to their assumptions of not being enough.

Your children begin to act out of control to gain attention that caused them to be labeled as a "behavioral problem child." However, their actions go unnoticed. An emotional identity crisis will cause your children to become depressed, unhappy, and suffer from trying to figure out your actions, thoughts, and withdrawals because of your "revolving doors."

Part-time fathers of the fatherless sons and daughters, it is pathetic that you all do not see that your revolving doors are a problem. The continuous cycle has to stop! It destroys your son's and daughter's identity. Man up, and take care of your children. As they become wiser and older you will not have anyone to blame but yourself when they are filled with resentment.

Part-time fathers of the fatherless children, you might not care now; but trust my word when I say, when you are old and gray you will, but then it will be too late.

Our sons and daughters are at war when they look at themselves in the mirror; when they are all alone; and as they look at other people and compare themselves. They ask themselves, who am I?

Challenges take them down as they try to define themselves; however, single mothers try their hardest to show and tell their children they are loved just the way they are. They are unique, beautiful, and handsome. Single mothers go above and beyond to fill the void that will always be a wound secretly opened.

My youngest son was bullied in Kindergarten through third grade. It tore me up inside, knowing my son was in deep pain mentally, emotionally, and physically. I fought hard for the bullying to end, although it took some years because children nowadays are so cold, and their parents aren't any better because they are filled with denial. It didn't stop me; they knew Charlena, Elijah's mother was not going to stop until something was done!

Elijah's father wasn't much help. He resides up north and he is a "revolving door" father; he's in and out every three to six months, and at times, years. I tried calling him to get his advice on the situation. Parenting doesn't come with a handbook on how to solve problems. I can say he tried, but by the advice that was given, I realized he didn't know his son at all. He didn't understand where I was coming from because, at that time, he hadn't seen Elijah in four years.

He talked to him every now and then. However, truth be told, although; he is Elijah's father and Elijah is his son—both of them were strangers to each other. Therefore, there was only so much he could do. Honestly, neither Elijah nor I could depend on him to help with the dreadful situation.

Revolving doors fathers, please know that you need to get to know your children. Understand their wants and needs, because every child is so unique in their own way. I am a firm believer that, when your children are young, that is the time to love on them as long and as hard as you can. When they are toddlers it amazes me how one minute they like certain foods, yet the next dislike what you thought was their favorite dish.

As they grow into their primary school years, it blows my mind how they outgrow their clothes so quickly! Not to mention, that during those "change their mind swiftly years" they are trying out new things here and there. Such as jumping from one sport to another, making friends, and hanging out as they are finding where they fit in.

During their "terrific" teen years, they are all over the place as they love to keep their parents tangled up with their wishy-washy ways. Ugh, got to love it! However, it is wonderful to participate in their accomplishments and be there for them for their downfalls. As they grow, they become their own individual person. Time doesn't wait on anyone. Take advantage and love on them as long as you can.

Father of the fatherless children, you are missing out on so many memories that would be cherished for a lifetime.

Although his father wasn't much help, I wished he could have been. As a mother, I believe a father's role is important; whether he resides in the state or not. A father's role is important because just as mothers are miracle workers, fathers have their special magic too!

When Elijah was bullied, it broke his spirit and ripped it to the core, inside and out. Mentality, he was always in a daze and not wanting to live. I had to seek help and watch him carefully because it was scary. It would have been amazing and a huge help if I'd had assistance from his father, but as a single mother, I had to run the show and be the groundbreaker. Indeed, I hit the ground running, and everyone was backed into a corner because my son's voice and mine were going to be heard. I did not take NO for an answer. It was all or none; and "none" wasn't on my agenda.

As a single mother, it is not easy taking care of the load alone. I had to let my son know he had someone in his life who would fight for him by any means necessary. As my son saw me on a daily basis fighting for him, his self-esteem was higher, stronger, and he became a fighter mentally, spiritually, emotionally, and if need be, physically. He never hesitated to let me know if someone bullied him because he knew I would turn my car around, march up to the school, and be his voice without hesitation.

It took time, but as months to years, I worked with my baby. We read self-help books together to raise our vibration through meditation. Every day, on our way to school we took time to say our affirmation: I am powerful, I am different, I am going to have a great day, I am positive energy, I am loved, I am happy, I am not going to let anyone steal my joy, peace, and happiness, etc. As time passed, my son revealed his identity and he called himself the "Marine Man."

I put him in self-defense classes such as Tae Kwon Do and Jiu-Jitsu. He took them very seriously, and his confidence was out of this world. I saw a significant change in my baby! His emotions were deepened as he knew words are just that... Words. I taught him that he could give life to those words or he could put them to rest. I loved hard on my baby because I wasn't going to lose my son due to craziness.

Each day, was a blessing because my baby was blossoming like a bed of colorful flowers. I wasn't going to let my son lose his identity to this senseless world. The fight was worth every worry and pain I carried for my baby, and I wouldn't have done anything differently.

Our sons and daughters question their identity when they are in their innocence, and it is up to us as parents to help mold our children with the truth. As they understand where they come from, they will form parts of their own identity, as they age and know what works and what doesn't work for them.

Fathers of the fatherless sons and daughters, your presence will help build your children's identity. Whether you know it or not, your presence builds security and confidence, and it will produce great strides in your children's confidence and determination.

However, fathers of the fatherless children, eliminating your presence or being a "revolving door," you are pulling your children under to the point that their confidence is shattered. Your children are unsure where they stand and feel out of place with the many different experiences they battle constantly. Their private thoughts are signs of not feeling wanted, loved, or accepted.

Single mothers have to console our sons and daughters to help them find an open path from their sense of loss. Single mothers are our children's "social role model" because we have to keep reminding them that in spite of their fathers being absent, we have unconditional love for them. However, I say again, fathers of the fatherless sons and daughters, single mothers cannot fill the open wound.

Fathers of the fatherless children, take off the blindfold and see that you are your son's and daughter's impediments. You are stealing their identity of what is rightfully theirs. I label you all as "Identity Thieves" because you all have caused a crime; your crime is robbing your children of happiness, feeling loved by you, and not giving them the opportunity to love you in return. You all have robbed your children of a chance at fully building their personality. Instead, they have unanswered questions that will linger on without a direct answer.

The blindfolds are thicker than I can possibly imagine because it's ridiculously crazy that you, the fathers of the fatherless sons and daughters cannot acknowledge that you all are identity thieves. You all complain that you do not have the money to help financially, but what about your time? Each breath you take consists of time. Sadly, for our sons and daughter, you make up excuses for your lack of time as well, yet you all become upset because you want all the glory and respect for doing nothing.

Fathers of the fatherless sons and daughters, when your children are older it never fails, you all want to step into their lives when the hard work is completed. Your lack of better judgment is so concealed with lies, you do not have the guts to admit you're wrong. As you become upset over your own doing, you want to point fingers at everyone but yourself. Why is that? How dare you think it is your children's fault? How can your lips form words and blame the single mother? You should be thanking her for raising your children without a single helping hand from you.

What makes matter worse is that the fathers of the fatherless sons and daughters all become so angry to the point that they want to cut their children out of their lives.

Reminder.

Wake up call.

Hello, can you hear me?

You've been there and done that already.

The cost the identity thieves have to pay—they never saw it coming.

Your sons and daughters put up their guard because their identity was stolen. As they freeze their emotions, they put on armor for protection. Your children erect firewalls because they are vulnerable and are proactive in their steps. They are very cautious because they do not want to be reminded of your broken promises. Therefore, their best defense is to protect themselves from avoiding falling victim to the shattered dreams you've caused.

Our sons and daughters who were once babies, toddlers, teenagers, young adults, and adults have made up their minds to settle for healing their own wounds. They are tired of your regular routine of being a sorry excuse and useless father. They made themselves a harder target so they are not attacked as the victim. They put a lock on their life because they refused to do hard time because of your actions. They do not deserve to be charged with a life sentence. Therefore, you are no longer able to violate and interrupt their peace of mind.

After their identity has been taken unwillingly, the recovery process begins to take place. As they accept your absence and unanswered questions, they calmly say, "Thank you, for nothing." They do not want the struggle of resentment, asking why over and over again. The damage is done. For some of our children, the wounds heal but for others, they cover it up with a waterproof band-aid. Father of the fatherless sons and daughters, your approval is no longer needed.

Let it be known, one day, you will need your sons and daughters. I hope for your sake they are willing to be there. If not, you need to look in the mirror, be honest with yourself as you tell yourself—you think you took the easy way out, but you cheated yourself of love, happiness, joy, and better yet, a well-deserved life with your child.

Know that your sons and daughters will be alright. They have their mothers who will not let them fall. They have strong mothers who will do anything for their babies; even give their life. Father of the fatherless children, you should be thankful that you did something right, you picked a woman who was strong enough to raise your sons and daughters alone.

Single mothers cannot do it all; one thing for sure, we try our best to heal our babies' wounds in any way possible. As we cradle our sons and daughters in our arms, we are molding them and shaping their identity because we are making strong warriors, even it if becomes the death of us.

Father of the fatherless sons and daughters, you should also want the best for your children. You've always been welcomed since day one (when they were conceived). However, it was your choice to be a part of their life or not.

Father of the fatherless children, it is time to change; and the time is now. You shouldn't want your sons and daughters to isolate themselves from the world because of your doing. You should want more for your children. You shouldn't want your sons and daughters to feel empty and alone because your presence never existed. You should want to be present and active in your children's lives.

Fathers of the fatherless children, we never said parenting would be easy. Look at your children, look deeply, and see your sons and daughters are an image and a part of you. You shouldn't let a part of "you" be the reason why they are defeated because of "you" their father. You should want them to be happy and proud that they have your blood and DNA running through their veins.

Father of the fatherless sons and daughters, you are the missing piece. Either you are going to man-up and fill that empty space in the puzzle or be a coward and take the easy way out.

Either way, when all is said and done, if you are in your son's and daughter's lives it will be a win-win situation for everyone. If you decide to walk away and it all goes up in flames, your sons and daughters will be the last ones standing!

3

The Root of the Problem

It is a shame that single mothers are living in poverty. There shouldn't be a reason why our children have to suffer because of the "lack of" not having what they need. Each day, a single mother has to make a decision about what has to be sacrificed to get through the day and/or maybe the month. Many times, a single mother has to play "catch up" on bills because her income isn't enough to pay all the bills and take care of her responsibilities.

Single mothers carefully decide which bills are important for the month. As if her schedule isn't busy enough, she has to figure something out, because all of the bills need to be paid. Her children need water, gas and/or electricity to stay warm, shower, and eat.

Somehow, some way or another, something has to give. That is the life of a single mother, something always has to give. All she does is "give." If a single mother needs assistance she has to go through hell and back to receive help.

She has to make a choice again. Something has to give again. Either she calls into her job, not being able to work her shift. Knowing she needs every penny. Or she seeks assistance, knowing there's a possibility she might not be approved. That's a risk she has to take; working her shift for today, or losing out on her hours that could have put money in her pocket. However, she knows she needs help; and that's a risk she's willing to take.

The choice is never easy. As she makes a critical decision to head to the Department of Family and Children Services Office, she finds that there's a long line filled with single mothers with worried looks on their faces. Either they have their children in a stroller, on their hip, or they are holding their hands.

The first time, I walked into the Department of Family and Children Services, I felt ashamed and embarrassed, but I knew I needed help. When I stepped foot in the door, all eyes were on me. I saw children with runny noses, shoes torn apart, and some of them didn't even have on a coat (it was cold outside). However, I am more than sure, every mother that was applying for assistance was doing the best she could do.

Each chair in the room had nasty stains as if it was dried-up poop, however, it was built-up dirt. Instead, I decided to sit on the floor because the floor was much cleaner than the chairs. "Is this your first time here?" a young girl asked me.

"Yes," I replied.

"Oh, well, you have to sign in at the front desk," she added.

"Thank you," I replied.

"You're Welcome," she said.

The room was filled with so many mothers who were in need of assistance. As I walked to the front desk, I was saying excuse me over and over again. I had to watch my step very carefully as there were children playing and sliding on the floor to keep themselves busy.

I walked to the front desk. A lady barely looked up. However, she didn't acknowledge my presence.

There were tons of pencils and clipboards on the counter.

"Take one of each," the lady said, without making eye contact.

"Excuse me?" I asked, humble and confused.

"Take one of each. Take one pencil. Take one clipboard," she said rudely.

I didn't say anything because I knew I needed assistance.

I took one pencil and clipboard.

As she gathered the paperwork, I held my hand out. She put a bright yellow paper on the counter because she didn't want to touch my hand.

I took the bright yellow paper off the counter. I walked away, sat on the floor, and filled it out.

I took the paper back and reached out to give it to her. "You can put it on the counter and I will get it," she said, without ever making eye contact.

I put it down and walked back to my corner.

Hours went by before my name was called. I filled the time by reading over my notes because I had an exam within two days.

Finally, my name was called, "Charlena. Charlena Jackson," a light but firm voice said.

I gathered my things, "Here." I answered.

The older lady was very polite and she held the door open for me. "Follow me," she said.

"How are you doing this morning?" she asked.

I was taken aback because of the rudeness from earlier. "I am doing well, thank you for asking. How are you doing?"

Her voice changed. It was like she never been asked how she was doing before. "I am fine now, thank you so much for asking."

She paused.

"You know, Charlena, it's a wonderful feeling when someone asks you in return how you are doing," she said with a huge smile on her face.

"It is a wonderful thing," I replied.

We walked into her cubical which had a nice view of the trees outside. "How can I help you?" she asked.

"I am here because I need assistance for myself and my children. Daycare, healthcare insurance, and food stamps," I replied.

She gathered my information and logged everything into the system.

"Umm," she murmured a couple of times.

She finally broke the silence. "I see you're working," she said as she looked at the computer screen.

"Yes. I am a work-study student," I replied.

"Oh," she said as her eyebrows arched.

"Umm, I see you own a car," she added.

"Yes. I do. A Mazda 626," I answered.

"I see that it is paid off," she said as she focused on the screen.

I wasn't sure what she was getting at. "Yes. It is. I paid it off last year," I answered.

"With what?" she asked out of curiosity.

"Well, I made monthly payments with my refund check from school," I replied.

"I see you are a student and receive government loans. What is your major?" she asked.

"Yes. I am in school. My major is biology," I answered.

"Biology," she repeated.

"Yes," I confirmed.

"So, you attend a university?" she asked, as her voice changed.

I was confused by her questions. "Yes. I attend a university," I answered slowly.

"Well, you are doing better than me. I haven't gotten the chance to go back to school," she remarked.

I sat there in silence as I looked at her.

"Well, Charlena, unfortunately, if you want assistance you would have to attend a technical school. The Government does not provide assistance to students who are in a university," she said, as her attitude changed.

To have an understanding of what she said I sat back in my chair and asked, "I cannot receive assistance because I am in college?"

"Technically, Charlena, you are not in college, you attend a university. Not to mention, you own your car and you work. The evidence that is provided here states that you are willing and able to provide for yourself and your children," she said with a smirk on her face.

I paused.

"Look on the bright side. You are doing better than me. You're working on your degree, and I have nothing," she continued sarcastically.

"Thank you, for your time," I said as I walked out of her cubicle.

There were so many things wrong in that conversation. It saddens me that a mother must be beyond her last hope in order to receive help. It is pathetic that a single mother is punished for trying to make a better life and living for her children. Let it be known, working, going to school, and taking care of my children (two at the time) wasn't easy.

The root of the problem is that the fathers of the fatherless children get a slap on the wrist for doing nothing. They are not held accountable for anything. Yet single mothers have to suffer to provide. We are told no we cannot receive assistant because we are trying to better ourselves. Goodness gracious, the picture is tainted.

Single mothers are judged and hear this statement all the time: "You knew what he was about before you slept with him." That could be true in a sense, but the reality is—people change as well. The person you met years ago turns out to be totally different from the person you know now.

How is it fair to put blame on the mother? How is it fair to even pass judgment? Asking for assistance shouldn't determine a mother's worth. A mother shouldn't be looked down upon as if she is a contagious disease. We, as single mothers, are trying the best we can without help from the fathers of the fatherless children. The root of the problem is so far from the truth, and it needs to be revised.

I waited about six months to reapply at a different location (the Department of Family and Children Services). After going through so much disrespect, hell, and paperwork, I finally was approved for assistance. However, in order to be approved; sadly, I had to cut down my hours at work, and since my mother was the co-signer on the car, I had to make sure the car was entirely in her name. I didn't drop out of school. However, in order to be approved for daycare and food stamps; I had to sign up for a government check.

I did whatever it took legally to receive assistance to make my load easier. All that I sacrificed was worth it because my children had more than enough food to eat, and I used the government check to pay for their clothes. What remained I used to pay my bills. Daycare was amazing because I didn't have to take my daughter to school with me (at that time she was a couple of months). I also had health insurance (Medicaid) which was a huge help.

I made the best of what I was given. I took advantage of the system and made it work for me. Although I had to put up with their rudeness every six months, I kept my mouth shut because I didn't want to burn any bridges. I knew I was doing this for my babies and myself to get ahead.

When my daughter was six years old her father had a mandatory court date. I called the Child Support Office for an update. I kid you not, when I say, I was on hold for four hours until a representative finally took my call. To pass the time, I cleaned the house, washed clothes, made dinner, picked my children up from school, went for a walk in the park to talk about our day, and helped them with their homework.

This wasn't the first time this issued occurred—one day, one of my classes was canceled and my children were at school. I called the Child Support Office to get an update on my case. Needless to say, I never had the chance to speak to anyone. I'm glad I had my charger handy. After waiting on hold for three hours—I was curious to see how long was I going to be holding to speak with a representative, therefore, I made the choice to hold on to seek an answer to my "curious" question. Pathetically, I was holding on from 9 a.m -5 p.m as if I was working an eight-hour shift (getting paid) just to hold the phone. To take advantage of the time—I ran a couple of errands (I waited in line to pay my power, water, and gas bill), went to the grocery store, iron my children's clothes for the remaining of the week, fixed their lunch, cooked dinner, studied, picked my children up from school, and spent time with them all while holding for a representative. When the clock struck 5 p.m. I was disconnected from the call. Needless to say, I am not going to say it was a waste of time. I would say, I've proven my case—when it comes to mothers needing assistance or getting an update for "making" the child's father pay little to nothing in child support—it is a tug-a-war.

Long story short, My daughter's father told the judge he made minimum wage (he brought his check for proof). Let me remind you, he was behind five thousand dollars in child support. The judge granted his wish to continue to pay the minimum which was two hundred and twenty-three dollars monthly. Sadly, I was on the phone for hours and couldn't reach anyone, however, my child's father made demands of what he couldn't do and his demands were granted. This picture here—is flawed and tainted in so many ways and on so many levels. Yet, the government states they seek the best interest for the children.

I was so angry! What can I do with two hundred and twenty-three dollars a month? How selfish on the father's and judge's part. I was speechless and highly disappointed. The judge (government) should be ashamed because I was getting more than that when I was receiving a government check.

I asked the Child Support Adviser, how could that be? As she and I looked through my file, we saw there were months and years he had gone without paying a penny. Several months he paid only one dollar and twenty-five cents. The most he ever paid monthly was forty-four dollars and some change. To add insult to injury, he told the judge he couldn't pay the minimum and to not suspend his driver's licenses.

The judge again granted his wish and put him in a Father Development Class. Basically, he got a slap on the wrist to continue to do nothing. What the fathers of the fatherless children and the judge fail to realize is that they are not hurting the mother; they are hurting the children. The children are going without; what can a child get from a Father Development Class. That is simply time being wasted, and an excuse to not pay child support. Especially since he made the choice to not be involved in his daughter's life since she was a couple of months old.

How is it that the fathers of the fatherless children can pay the minimum in child support and that is fine with the state. In reality, the state doesn't care; the judges basically says it is not their problem. Two-hundred and twenty-three dollars! How in the world is a mother supposed to support her children with that? That is not enough money for daycare, afterschool care, food, clothes, shoes, not to mention if your child has special needs such as speech or disability, and/or extra activities (soccer, cheerleading, tennis, etc.) Is it fair that the mother has to do the best with what she is given and still work her butt off to make ends meet? What is given is not even half of her check. Yet, the fathers of fatherless children continue to live life without any worries or responsibilities.

The root of the problem is neglected by the judges (government) because they do not care; they are trying to get through as many files as possible during the day. They do not take the child's well-being into consideration.

Three years later, my daughter turned nine years old. I asked for my child support case to be revised. I was asked by her father to take a DNA test to stall for time. The test came back that he was 99.9 percent the father (which I knew, and he knew it too). Years passed and I called to receive an update. I was told by the Child Support Representative that he has to take care of himself first in order to provide child support. Towards the end of the conversation, she said the child support revision is still pending.

Eight years later, my daughter is seventeen years old and the request is still pending.

The root of the problem will never be resolved unless the court system looks out for the best interest of the children.

However, their best interest for the children has a different definition. There are mothers who are in a domestic violence relationship who ask for help, yet it goes unheard and ignored by the system, but the voices of the fathers of the fatherless children are heard when they do not have enough money to pay child support. However, they "say" they're looking out for the best interest of the child. How so?

There are mothers who worked two or three jobs to keep up with the bills, receiving nothing or very little in child support. Some mothers do not have support from family or friends, therefore, they will leave their children at home with their oldest child. In some states, it is forbidden. It depends on the age (which is understandable); however, there are mothers who leave their children at home with their fifteen-year-old who are charged with neglect because they had to work the night shift. What is a mother supposed to do when support is limited?

Most of the time, when the mothers apply for government assistance, they are not eligible for assistance from the government Childcare and Parent Services (CAPS). They are turned away because they make too much money from their minimum-wage 9-5 job, which is why some mothers work two or three jobs to have enough to get by.

Yet, the mother is charged with child abandonment because she trusted her fifteen-year-old to watch over her children at night (because she thought they would be sleeping) while she works.

After she gets off the graveyard shift, she will go home, cook breakfast, get her children together for school; and take them to school as she gets a couple of hours in for her next shift. How is the mother charged with child abandonment and child cruelty while the father of the fatherless children has no penalties or consequences to pay? That is a deep-rooted problem that needs to be analyzed.

How is it abandonment if a mother lets her fifteen-year-old stay home with the children for a couple of hours so she can make it to her second job on time to provide for her children? When she comes home, a social worker is at her house, picking up her kids, and/or the mother is taken to jail for trying to support her children.

A mother does the best she can; however, the odds are not in her favor. A single mother will be charged for neglect if her child has on dirty clothes, or if the child says he/she didn't have enough food to eat last night. The mother will be charged with neglect because the lights or water were off until her next check comes within two weeks.

The mother goes through so much and gets so little. How is that fair? The root of the problem is buried, clearly overlooked, and ignored.

The fathers of the fatherless children are the ones who abandon and neglect their sons and daughters. They are not held responsible for their part in regards to helping raise their children. Where is the justice for our sons and daughters? Father of the fatherless children, you are a sorry excuse for a man.

Single mothers, where do we go from here? We have asked ourselves times and time again, how do we fly without wings? How do we fight without armor? How do we survive with little to nothing?

We must continue to fight for our children with our voices and actions. It hurts, and God knows, it's hard to breathe most days. We cannot, and we must not lose the will to fight. We are our children's purpose and future. We cannot lose hope. We must count our suffering as joy. It is because of us (the single mothers) that our children have wings to fly. It is because of single mothers that our sons and daughters have hope for a new day. Their dreams that will form into reality and the smiles on their faces are like music to our ears.

Nobody can feel our pain, nor do they care to hear our cry. However, our children's laughter brings us so much joy and makes us realize why we work as hard as we do.

The fathers of the fatherless children, government, judges, and child support agencies have cold, cold hearts. However, I have good news, single mothers! I do know this will not, and cannot, go on forever because our children are our future, and everyone who's in a position of power right now will one day have to step down from the podium.

Single mothers, we have to raise our children to take a stand and change the world. After all, in time, the world will be theirs to carry and change. Therefore, a change is coming sooner than we think.

Do not give up, keep the faith, and know that as single mothers, we have what it takes to survive.

4

Chief Guardian

Heads of households nowadays are being run by a healthy percentage of Chief Guardians. The Chief Guardian takes up multiple roles and wears many hats. She's a leader and a groundbreaker. As she makes her struggles appear effortless, so she can gain strength to survive the next minute of the day.

The Chief Guardian is a warrior as she juggles different responsibilities all at once; trying to keep a steady pace as she balances one foot in front of the other. The Chief Guardian is fearless because she is the Queen that has to prepare for a battle against the unknown situations that occur on a daily basis.

The Chief Guardian is filled with amazing, unbelievable strength, perseverance, and wisdom. She is powerful, she is the disciplinarian, she is a survivor, she is victorious – and most importantly, she is a mother.

The mother is not only the Chief Guardian of the household; however, she is the Chief Guardian in her children's lives, as the father of the fatherless children is either no longer in his children's lives, whether he simply comes and goes as he pleases, is deceased, or incarcerated.

The Chief Guardian dives deep and pulls strength from all the hardship and struggles that are thrown at her, yet she is blamed for everything that has gone wrong. Not only is she blamed for everything, but she is also always judged by her actions. As she's being blamed and judged she's always given a shitty stick and dealt an unfair hand. How is that fair to the Chief

Guardian? She is the one who has to carry the load when she doesn't have any fight left. She is the one who has to figure every burden out, without any help from the fathers of the fatherless children. Yet she finds the courage to figure it out as she keeps pushing and moving on through the pain.

There are times when the Chief Guardian complains. However, it is for a short moment because she realizes that whether she complains or not, the show must go on. On a daily basis, the Chief Guardian puts on her armor. She is unstoppable, her mind is focused on all of the responsibilities she has to execute.

Sadly, when it comes to the Chief Guardian there is no room for error. However, we are not as perfect as everyone thinks we should be. We are human. We are allowed to make mistakes. We do the best we can as the load piles up and we embrace each step to carry everything that is given and thrown at us. Just like the blood in our veins, we flow gracefully because giving up isn't an option.

When I applied for assistance at the Department of Family and Children Services, I was told I couldn't receive any assistance because I was attending a university. In order to receive assistance, I would have to drop out of school and enroll in a Technical Institution. That wasn't an option for me, so I took a chance to speak with my professor about my situation.

I was surprised by his response, "Charlena, if you like, your three-month-old daughter is welcome to join our lecture," he said as he smiled.

I sat there silently, my eyes filled with tears because I was used to hearing the word no. My professor gave me a hug. "Charlena, it is going to be okay. Normally, I wouldn't allow children in my classroom, but your determination inspires me. You have a drive. I wish my children had, and they do not have any responsibility. You should be proud of yourself," he said as he gave me some tissue to wipe my face.

Tears were flowing down my cheeks. "I do not know what to say," I said as I tried to catch my breath.

My professor's eyes were filled with tears as well. "Do not make me cry, Charlena," he said as he wiped away the tears before they fell from his eyes.

I couldn't stop crying. "Thank you. Thank you so much. I am beyond grateful."

The very next day, I had my bookbag on my back, my daughter's baby bag on my right shoulder, and my daughter on my left hip.

When I walked in the classroom my professor was setting up a playpen. An ocean of tears streamed from my eyes. I felt like a child on Christmas day!

Although I had to step out of the class more than half of the time because my daughter was giving me a hard time, I recorded my lectures and listened to them as I put my children to bed at night.

Until this day, I am forever grateful that my professor gave me an opportunity to attend my lectures. I completed the quarter and passed all my classes!

As Chief Guardians, we have a choice to give up and give in or do what we have to do to survive.

Every single day, Chief Guardians roll the dice; praying and hoping that things will work out in our favor. As we ask for a little mercy, it is granted every now and then. One minute we, as Chief Guardians, have it all together as we come up for a breath of fresh air. However, the next challenge creeps up out of nowhere. Without warning, we have to quickly gasp for air and find the strength to swim through the aggressive waves.

Chief Guardians are very successful at hiding the hurt, frustration, pain, and our worries. We do whatever it takes to lighten our loads. However, most of the time, we have to put some of our baggage aside as we focus on what's important at the present time. There are bags we have laid down for a while, but you better believe we have to go back to gather them up again to figure out how to proceed as we move forward.

Chief Guardians are fighters. We do the unbelievable, unexpected, and make the impossible, possible! There is no way, we are going to let anyone defeat us when it comes to our children. When we hit the ground, we get right back up and run the unknown course that lies ahead.

I was told over and over again that my little one was on track with regard to his speech pattern. However, as time passed, it was hard for me to understand his words.

I took him to the doctor to be examined multiple times. Once again, the physician reassured me everything was just fine. As a mother, I wasn't content with the words "just fine" because I knew otherwise.

I made another appointment. One of the physicians looked over my little one's medical records, "Ms. Jackson, I have great news! Everything is A.O.K! Why do you worry so much?" she asked as she smiled.

"I am not worried. I am a concerned mother who sees what you all do not see. I am with my son on a daily basis. I read peer-review articles, and I've been observing my son's speech patterns. No, everything is not A.O.K. His speech is impaired. Do you think I want something to be wrong with my son on purpose?" I asked, with great concern.

"Ms. Jackson, every parent wants a healthy child. However, I am telling you, your son is okay," she said calmly, with a little frustration in her voice.

"And I am telling you, yes, he is healthy, but he has a speech impairment pattern. I am his mother. I know when something is wrong with my son. To save all of us some time, please write me a referral to a Speech Pathology Specialist. After they examine my son, we all can take it from there. I cannot and will not rest until I have some answers." I said in a calm, firm, and concerned voice.

"Ms. Jackson, I agree with you. I am going to write a referral so we all can be at peace. You will see that you were worried about nothing the entire time." She smiled as she approved my little one to be examined by a speech pathologist.

"Thank you," I replied.

When I left the doctor's office, I made an appointment with the speech pathologist, and they saw my little one the very next day.

Long story short, they performed a couple of exams. The end results were: my son had a lot of fluid in his ears and many unknown ear infections. I was surprised because he never ran a fever or pulled on his ear, etc., which is why, when he spoke, he sounded like he was speaking as if he was underwater. Thankfully, the fluid didn't damage his hearing; however, it damaged his speech patterns. We started treatment right away.

After his doctor's office received his results, they apologized for their misdiagnosis. Without hesitation, I accepted their apology. However, I let it be known that they need to take what the parents say seriously. After all, we are with our children on a daily basis, and we only want what's best for them.

Although my little one's father was a "revolving door" father, I called him to let him know what was going on with our son. I wasn't surprised by his insensitive reaction. "Charlena, our son does not have a speech problem. You want something to be wrong with him. He will be labeled. This will follow him throughout his life and he will be in special classes at school."

"Our son has a speech disability. He needs professional help or he will suffer and be behind in school as he gets older," I replied, trying to help him understand.

"No. He does not have a disability, Charlena," he argued. He sounded upset.

"You know what? I do not know why I even called you. You do not know our son. You haven't seen him in years but I try my best to keep you posted about what goes on in his life. Honestly, you do not care, because you do not take the time to get to know him. The least you can do is say thank you for putting effort into helping our child. However, you are in denial like always. I see some things never change," I said angrily.

I didn't give him a chance to respond. I hung up the phone.

What made me angry was that his father didn't understand I had to put up a fight for over a year to make sure our son received the proper treatment he needed.

It's been eight years. My son has come a long way and his speech is getting better and better every single day!

It never amazes me how much we are overlooked as Chief Guardians. What I love about all the Chief Guardians in the world is; we will not settle for the word "no." If we know something can be done, we make sure we successfully overcome every obstacle. That way, we do not leave room for anyone to say, "You have to do this, and do that, or you forgot this, or you forgot that." No, we made sure all of the "this and that" was completed.

I admire us as Chief Guardians. We are always underestimated. People always have something to say, but they are not willing to jump in the deep, unknown troubled waters. However, we as Chief Guardians, never hesitate to jump in the troubled waters when it comes to our children. We take that leap – with or without a life jacket!

As Chief Guardians, we are survivors! We manage to take each and every last cross we're carrying up the steep rocky hill! We never ask for the mountains to be moved out of our way; we stand there for a short minute, look at the distance we have to travel as we say, "Here we go; it's all or none." As Chief Guardians, as I stated before when it's time to suit up for war the word "no" is not in our vocabulary.

We have our moments when we carry too much at one time, therefore, our minds begin to form doubts when we tumble down full speed as we try to search for the breaks. Sometimes the breaks are nowhere to be found, so when we tumble, we tumble hard and hit the ground even harder.

We are bruised from tumbling non-stop. It hurts. It's painful. It's frustrating. As we lie down and collect our thoughts, we want to give in, but we know that is not possible. We get up, dust ourselves off, pick up our crosses and head back up the hill. This time, we take a different approach. We know it will not be easy, but we are not foolish enough to take the same route twice.

One thing, I love about we as Chief Guardians is—when we are tumbling down the hill we are not thinking about the aggressive hits. Our adrenaline is at an all-time high as we think about what we have to complete on our agenda and what's next. Before the rough tumble, we were stressed, but after the tumble, it cured our emotional trauma. We suit up and say, "Here we go. We have to and will get up this mountain because there isn't away around it or through it; the only way to go is up."

Chief Guardians take on the responsibilities of being both the mother and father. I've noticed that a lot of people say, a mother can't be a father. That could be very well true, however, we do not have a choice but to "play" the "father role" to the best of our ability. We are the mothers, but the fathers of the fatherless children cowardly volunteer our services. It's hard enough being a mother, but it is harder trying to play the "father's" role as well. However, those are the cards we were dealt. I can say, for the sake of the matter—no, we do not know how to be a "father," but we do the best we can. That is why it is imperative that all fathers take responsibly and execute their role full-time.

It is important that Chief Guardians have financial help from the fathers of the fatherless children. As Chief Guardians, we struggle at times to take care of our children with only one source of income. I am proud to say, by the grace of the Great Divines, we make it happen. We make it look easy, but please know, fathers of the fatherless children, it is not easy. We, as Chief Guardians, know how to balance our options to keep the bills paid, put food on the table, clothe our children, and take care of our children to the best of our ability.

Fathers of the fatherless children, there is a message for those who pay child support of a dollar and some pennies. A couple of dollars randomly covers the minimum that is "required" for you to pay, and for those who do not pay anything at all. Ask yourself, how is that fair to your sons and daughters? Do you not think your children want to participate in extracurricular activities? Sadly, the fathers of the fatherless children, all think that what little money they send is being spent by us, the mothers, on ourselves.

As for Chief Guardians like myself, I use every penny on my children. My needs and wants are not on the list, and if I do something for myself with the money I earned, I feel guilty for buying clothes or a pair of shoes after a year or so because of wear and tear. Needless to say, I have the same clothes in my closet from years ago. I prefer to use my money on my children to keep them busy in extracurricular activities. These activities keep their minds focused on the good, and gives them hope knowing they are good at something. It keeps them out of trouble and busy in a positive and productive way.

With that being said, my youngest son's father pays the minimum in child support, which is two-hundred and twenty-three dollars monthly. That is not enough for clothes, shoes, after-school care for one week, or extracurricular activities. What is beyond ridiculous is that when my son visited his father up north, he told me his father had a closet filled with clothes as if it was a department store. Boxes and boxes of shoes were stacked up against each other along the wall at both ends of his closet. The top rack in his closet was neatly lined and filled with many hats. Last, but not least, his dresser was covered with watches, and sunglasses of many colors and different brands.

When his father decided to visit my son a couple of years later, he was wearing Jordan's from head to toe. Yet he only pays the minimum in child support! It never fails to amaze me how the fathers of the fatherless children put themselves first – and their children are the least of their concerns.

As a Chief Guardian working my ass off supporting my children and myself, it makes me mad how fathers take the easy way out. It angers me how they live life every day, not knowing or caring about how their child is doing. Not knowing if their child is alive or dead or if they are hungry or have full stomachs. They careless about their child's favorite color, favorite sport, subject, or how they are doing in school, etc.

When my youngest son's father came to visit, he brought my son a pair of pants, four short-sleeved shirts, two long-sleeved shirts, a couple of pairs of shorts, underwear, and some socks. I might add, that was the first time in four years he came to visit. If I was waiting on him to clothe my son, my son would be naked. If I was waiting on him to feed my son, he would be deceased due to starvation and thirst.

The Chief Guardian has to put up with so much, yet in return, we either get little scraps or nothing. The load is completely ours to carry.

Fathers of the fatherless sons and daughters, your children deserve nothing less than your best. They deserve to have your love, support, and your presence in their life full-time.

Chief Guardians shouldn't have to take on the load alone. It would be a wonderful thing if you all, the father of the fatherless children, stepped up to the plate, were active, and made a home run in your children's life. As a Chief Guardian, trust me when I say, you are missing out on so much. Our children say and do some of the cutest things, and they are precious. Memories last a lifetime, and you should want to be a part of those memories; as opposed to being invisible.

Chief Guardians, we are incredible!

Chief Guardians, we are magnificent!

I know it is not easy, but by being in our son's and daughter's lives we are their Shero's. We are leading by example. They recognize our hard work and dedication. I am more than sure, our sons and daughters will make us proud.

Keep the wheels in motion, for we will not give up on our children, we will be there for our sons and daughters until the end of their journey, and they will appreciate us every step of the way!

5

Blame Game

When a child is in the middle of a sour and bitter relationship, they are the ones who tend to receive the short end of the stick. When there is resentment between the child's parents, the child is the one that suffers from the mark their parents placed on each other. Constantly, the child hears over and over again, "It is your mother's fault." Or, "It is your father's fault."

Yet the parents do not understand the child's mind is moving internally like a train that doesn't have breaks. Parents neglect to see that their child is screaming on the inside; nevertheless, their mind is like a ticking bomb filled with mixed emotions. Just because your child is quiet—it doesn't mean everything is okay. That is when parents need to dig deep and hear their children's silent cry.

When parents argue children may think at times that they are the reason for the argument. Sometimes they shut down and at times are afraid to speak up. Parents have to understand, sometimes we are the reason why our children stumble and/or trip and fall. Parents need to be the bigger person to not let our children get involved in our disagreements and to be mindful of our children before they fall in the midst of our problems. They should not feel like they are to blame because their parents cannot put their differences aside.

As parents, we have to learn that we cannot tip the scale when it comes to raising our children when both parents are not together. It is common to hold some sort of bitterness when one parent has moved on from the relationship. I see this often; some mothers hold their children hostage from the fathers who are trying to be a part of their son's and daughter's lives because he started to see someone else. Mothers, that is unacceptable. If your child's father wants to be in his son's or daughter's life full-time, give him the opportunity. After all, what went on between you and him isn't your child's problem. Therefore, it is wise to put your differences aside for your child's sake.

My ex-husband sent me a text and told me he was getting married. I was happy for him. However, he caught me off guard and asked me could our son be in his wedding. I told him no because he hasn't seen our son in years; and all of a sudden, he wants him to be in his wedding. He was very upset and he didn't understand my point of view. He claimed that I was keeping him away from our son; which wasn't true. I never met his fiancé a day in my life, and as a matter of fact, I never knew he was dating (which wasn't my business). The fact of the matter is, my son knew of his father, but he didn't know his father.

After he got married, my son's father asked me if Elijah could come up north for a visit. I told him no, because he hasn't reached out to Elijah, and our son doesn't know him. Again, he didn't understand. He played the blame game and said, "Charlena, why are you keeping me away from my son?" I explained to him that I wasn't keeping him away. I am not going to send my son somewhere where he doesn't know anyone, and he will be and feel alone. Again, he blamed me for all of his past mistakes.

I compromised with him and said, "How about this—you and your wife can come down south. She and I can get to know each other; therefore, I can put a name to a face and vice versa. By the way, what is your wife's name?"

"At the moment, Charlena, my wife's name isn't important." He replied.

I laughed slightly and said, "Okay. As a mother, I will be able to get a feel for her vibe; and she will be able to see and get to know Elijah—and he can do the same."

"No, you do not need to meet my wife. You do not need to know her name, and she does not need to see you, either." He replied.

"Let me put it this way, if Elijah and I cannot meet your wife then my son will not fly up north. I do not think it is a stretch for you all to travel to Georgia to see your son. Like always, you have an open invitation. Take it or leave it; it's up to you."

He continued to go back and forth as if I was the one at fault. I didn't break a sweat of frustration. I calmly said, "Okay. Well, when you all want to come see Elijah, then let me know ahead of time. Have a good day."

A couple of months later, Elijah's father came to visit; however, his wife didn't come. I never met his wife. Needless to say, I do not even know her name.

If pointing fingers, talking badly about me and blaming me for what he lacked made him feel good about himself, he could have at it. One thing I knew for sure, I wasn't going to send my son up north by himself for him to be alone with strangers. It's sad to say, but his father is a stranger to him because he is a revolving door father who feels as though everything should work out in his favor when he feels like he wants to be "father of the year" for an event, for a day, or for a couple of hours.

Reality check to the fathers of the fatherless children – fatherhood is never an off-duty job. It is all or nothing. Either you are in or you are out. Most importantly, father of the fatherless children, please know and hear me out clearly, it is not about you. You all need to start taking into consideration what's best for your children.

A couple of years passed. I spoke with Elijah's father and told him, if he's willing, we can compromise, work together, and co-parent for Elijah's sake. He agreed. I told him to feel free to Skype or Facetime Elijah anytime. I must say, for a couple of months we were getting along very well as co-parents. I was telling him what was going on in Elijah's life, and Elijah called and talked to him more than before. However, when his father asked could Elijah come up north to visit, he disliked my answer. Again, I told him no, because they've been talking on the phone for only a few months. I advised him to come down to Georgia to spend more time with Elijah face-to-face. He was very upset, blamed me and accused me of keeping his son from him.

I never understood what he wanted from me. As a mother, I was looking out for the best interests of my son. However, sadly, Elijah's father didn't understand.

I asked Elijah did he want to visit his father alone. Elijah replied, "No, because I am not comfortable. If he comes to see me, I would like for you to be there."

I tried telling his father what Elijah expressed to me. His father said, "Whatever, Charlena, this is all your doing. You are putting words in his head."

I never put words in my son's head. I knew he was Elijah's father; however, Elijah only knew of him, but he didn't fully know him enough to be comfortable around him alone.

A week before Thanksgiving, Elijah's father called and asked if he could come to see Elijah. I told him we were going on vacation. However, he could come during Christmas break if he like. Once again, he didn't understand. He blamed me for keep Elijah away. I explained to his father, he cannot expect me to cancel my vacation just so he can see Elijah, not to mention at short notice. I explained to him, we have to make plans ahead of time. I politely said, "If you want to come during Christmas, fine. We can plan for that, but please let me know. That way, I will know what we are doing for Christmas." His father didn't come for Christmas, nor did he send him anything for Christmas or his birthday.

I went back and forth with my son's father for a while. Until one day, I said to myself, this is draining. It is draining when a person doesn't understand. Regardless of what you say, they either chose not to understand or refuse to see the truth. Either way, I know I tried.

As a mother, I had to look out for the best interest of my child. I also extended multiple invitations numerous times for him to visit; therefore, he would have been able to form a bond with his son.

Father of the fatherless children, there is one thing you have to understand—forming a bond takes time. Just because you've talked to your child for a month or two straight over the phone doesn't mean he/she is comfortable and ready to spend time alone with you. I must say, though, talking to them over the phone is a start! However, time is of the essence; time doesn't wait on anyone, time is precious and time changes either for the better or for the worse. Take time out to get to know your children, and once they are comfortable, they will let their mother know when they are ready to spend time with you alone.

Mothers, do not rob your children of having both parents in their life. Co-parenting is possible. When your child is present, be respectful towards each other, get along for the moment, and when your child isn't in your presence, try to resolve the situation and know you all have to be in each other's life because your child deserves to have both parents.

Your children shouldn't have to suffer because of your personal issues towards each other. If the father of your children moved on, that is his choice. However, I do understand, if he dates a different woman every month or so, and you do not want your children to be briefly exposed to a different woman each time. That is not healthy for the child. With that being said, the father needs to respect your wishes and spend quality time with his children alone until he's in a stable permanent relationship.

However, if the father of your child gets married, it is only right and fair that you give him and his wife a chance at getting to know you and your child. If you get a chance to meet his wife, and you know she will take care of your child as her own, it is only fair that you do what is best for your child.

I know that this is easier said than done. It is a work in progress. However, if the mother and father respect each other, each other's boundaries, and what is asked of each other, the process will be able to move forward within time. Therefore, anything is possible, and things will adjust as they fall into place if both mother and father work together raising their children.

I am not perfect, but I try to look out for the best interests of my children. Before the above story took placed my ex-husband left my children and me. He decided he wanted to see the children a year after he left. I was a bitter, angry, frustrated, and fierce mad woman.

After he left, I didn't have anything. I had to start from ground zero. I was kicked out of my home, taking classes to receive assistance, working, going to school, and taking care of my children. I was at an all-time low. I felt like I was never ever going to rise again. Life had me on lockdown and I was suffocating. Depression and stress clouded my mind with fear and doubt. I was running on empty. I found hope in my children and looking at my babies every single day gave me the strength to push through the day.

I begged my husband to come back home so we could make it work; and/or at least come back to save the house so my children and I could have somewhere to stay. Over and over again, he said he wasn't ready. He decided to stay up north and live with his mother and Pops. A year passed, and he wanted to see the children. I was filled with rage. He really thought it was that easy to come back while I struggled the entire time.

I let him come down to see the children. When I saw his face, my heart was hurting, my blood was boiling, and my thoughts were blocked. Anger took over. I was a woman scorned in so many ways I couldn't imagine. He acted as if he hadn't done anything wrong. He walked up the apartment stairway that my children and I were staying in (the projects) and didn't think anything of the trash, bullet caps, broken glass from beer bottles, yellow tape near the far left, and leftover butts all over the ground.

A couple of guys were sitting and smoking on the steps as I said excuse me. One guy said, "What's up, man?" to my ex-husband. The guy was eyeing him because once again he had on all Jordan's (Jordan's shoes, socks, shorts, shirt, and hat). He had on a nice-looking watch and expensive shades.

As he was holding my little one, we walked in the door. "Charlena, you said you brought my clothes with you. Do you still have them?" he asked.

You could say, I was crazy for packing his clothes after he left me with nothing. I was hurt, but it was in my heart to do the right thing. Therefore, I had packed his clothes and put them in a black garbage bag.

"Yes, they are in the hallway closet," I replied.

He pulled out four huge black bags.

"Did you pack my shoes?" he asked.

I looked at him as I was shaking my head and said, "Yes, they are in the closet too."

He pulled out two black bags filled with shoes.

"I do not see my floor rug?" he said.

I was saying to myself, *are you kidding me?*

"I sold the floor rugs, washer, and dryer," I said, my blood boiling like lava.

"What you mean, you sold it?" he asked, as if he forgot he was the one that up and left me and the kids with nothing, to stay with his mother.

"I sold everything I could get money from. I had to survive. The kids and I had to eat. You wouldn't know anything about that. You left, remember? When the going got rough, you left your family to fend for ourselves. So, yes, I sold it because I needed money. You didn't send anything. You didn't come back to save the house. You left us in the cold while you were sipping on chili in a warm cozy house while we were freezing. You know what? I am not about to do this shit today. Get your shit. The least you can do is say, thank you for packing your shoes and clothes after you left." I said, trying to stay calm, but I couldn't take his ungrateful ass anymore.

"I do not want to talk about this," he said as he walked away.

He gathered his bags and asked me could the kids spend the night with him at the hotel. I wanted to say no. I was the one who struggled and was still struggling. He didn't bring the kids any clothes, food or anything. I was so angry. However, I couldn't make the situation about me. I had to be the bigger person for my children. I let the kids spend the night with him at the hotel.

The next day, he spent time with them, dropped them off, and traveled back up north without putting a dime in my pocket.

Is hard putting your differences aside, especially when the other person can't see they're wrong. I never got an apology for the dirty cards he played. It was a hard, dry, and bitter pill to swallow, but it wasn't about me. I did it for my children.

A week passed, and he called me with a lot of nonsense, "Charlena, I do not understand why you want to keep me from my son?" (My oldest children weren't his biological children; however, he was in my son's life when he was five years old and my daughter's life when she was eighteen months old).

"Excuse you, do you not remember you were the one who left and stayed away for over a year? I asked you to come back home. You always said you weren't ready. I dare you to play the victim." I hung up the phone in his face. He took the easy way out while I struggled with a five-month-old, a six-year-old and a ten-year-old. I was so angry because I was the one who had to figure everything out on my own.

A month or so passed, and he was still singing the same old song, that I was keeping him away from his son.

I put my pain aside and came up with a visitation plan. It was hard for me to let my children out of my sight. It was even harder to be the bigger parent because I felt like he was winning. I felt like he was getting everything. He disappeared for over a year, left the kids and I stranded, playing the victim, jumped right back out of the clear blue sky and wanted me to accommodate his needs while I suffered in deep pain emotionally, physically, mentally, spiritually, and financially. It was so easy for him to come right back in and get everything he didn't work hard for.

The plan I came up with hurt me to the core, but again, I put my feelings aside for my children. For two years my children went up north for spring break, summer break, and we alternated holidays. Two years, I missed my daughter's birthday and one year I was without my children for Christmas.

Within the two years the plan was in motion I received little to nothing financially. However, when my children visited him up north, I sent him money for food, clothes, etc. My children told me he bought beer with the money I sent. My children called me nearly every day, telling me they didn't eat breakfast or dinner.

My oldest son, who was twelve years old at the time, called me, saying he was babysitting a six-month-old baby, a nine-year-old, my daughter who was eight years old, and my little one who was nearly two years old, while my ex-husband and his cousin went to work or hung out. I was on fire! I called them and let them have it; not to mention, told them I was calling the police and I hoped they got back to the house before the police did.

My ex-husband made things so complicated. He would call me, telling me over and over again that I was keeping him from his son. I told him that was nonsense because of the visitation plan I came up with, which was fair on both ends.

That wasn't enough for him. He wanted my son to go up north alone without my oldest children. After the babysitting issue, I didn't agree. Although, my oldest children looked at him as a father, because my ex-husband was the only father they ever knew. My ex-husband said he wasn't responsible for Xavier and Sarah. I was crushed; and to add insult to injury, he said, "I do not want to be their father anymore." He told my eight-year-old daughter he was only Elijah's father (which she knew, and she knew of her biological father, but he wasn't in her life). How could a man tell a child that, knowing he's been in her life since the age of eighteen months? How cold.

I didn't let Elijah go up there alone, because I was afraid his father would try to kidnap my son and that I wouldn't ever see him again. In order for him to visit alone, it would have to be a court order, not on my terms of a "visitation plan."

When I told him that, he was very upset, but I wasn't going to accommodate his temper tantrum this time around.

A year passed, and he distanced himself.

I went to the courthouse to file some paperwork, only to find out my ex-husband had secretly tried to file for custody of Elijah. They served the papers to the apartment we were once living in; however, we had moved into a beautiful home; therefore, I wasn't served any papers. The clerk made a copy of the documents, and she said, "Wow, you look shocked, you didn't know anything about it at all, I see."

No, I didn't have a clue. I was taken aback, he was and always will be shifty. I knew from that day forth, I couldn't and wouldn't ever trust him again.

It wasn't just the fact that he'd filed the papers. It was the principle of the matter, he did it in a sneaky way. I was so mad, because how dare he tried to file for custody when he'd left us? He became a revolving door father, and I gave him every opportunity to be a real father (full-time). Just because he didn't get his way, he wanted to secretly sneak around.

After the case closed, I told him that I knew what he was up to; and how low down and dirty he was.

Things weren't ever the same after that.

The fathers of the fatherless children are so good at playing the "blame game." They blame the single mother for everything, and they never attempt to do a thing.

The fact that the fathers of the fatherless children have parents who chose to justify and accommodate their son's wrong doesn't make it any better. Until this day, I can never understand, how the parents (grandparents) of the fathers of the fatherless children cover their son's sorry asses. How can someone cover for a grown man, knowing they are wrong? Why would they lie for their children, knowing their grandchildren are suffering? What on the Great Divines earth is going through the grandparent's minds? Goodness.

Before and after my ex-husband left, his mother interfered in many ways. The situation was horrible when he left, I called her house. She wouldn't put him on the phone. She would either say he was in the shower, not there or plain out no, you cannot talk to him. What made matters worse, she said, "Do not call my boy anymore, you ran him down to the ground. Your children are not my boy's children, and the baby might not be his either."

I lost all respect for her and told her, "It's your fault that your son is a momma's "boy!" He's a grown man, and you're still breastfeeding him. You need to let him grow up and be a man. Our marriage wasn't your business. You are the reason why your "boy" is weak!"

When my children were visiting my ex-husband up north, they told me his mother treated them badly. When Christmas came around, she would give her biological grandchildren expensive gifts and gave my children (including my little one who is her biological grandson) socks and white t-shirts. Which was fine with me, because something is better than nothing.

However, from a child's standpoint, that was hurtful and so wrong.

His mother was so nasty – to the point that she gave all the children their gifts at the same time. That was so wrong, viewing it from a child's eyes (that is another reason why they didn't go back to visit).

Where is the love and respect for their grandchildren? Goodness, why can't the fathers of the fatherless children's parents see that their actions (along with those of their son) hurt their grandchildren? I feel as though a parent should tell their son the truth so he can either take responsibility or grow old with regrets.

Another "blame game" that never fails. The children's mother trusts the grandparents to look after their grandchildren when they are in their care. However, the grandparents will call their son over to take the children to spend the day with him. What makes matters worse, the grandparents tell their son to, "Make sure you bring the child back on time." That way, the mother will think the child has been in their care the entire time.

After the mother finds out, the grandparents are not allowed to see their grandchildren because of their sneaky move. The grandparents violated the mother's trust and lose out on seeing their grandchildren. Parents of the fathers of the fatherless children… Is it worth it?

Jasmine, a friend of mine was in this situation. After she dropped her daughter off and left her in the care of her grandmother (father's mother) she told her it was okay for Lee (her daughter's father) to come see her, but not to let him take her out of her care alone because he was charged for having a DUI multiple times, and he had a warrant out for his arrest.

Jasmine was hanging out with a couple of friends at Red Lobster. She looked over and saw her daughter in a high chair, eating spaghetti and sipping on some juice. Next to her was her daughter's father and a lady she had never met.

One of the most common roots of the problem of the blame game is the grandparents. Most of the time, it is the mother of the son that causes the most issues by always making excuses for her son's actions. Instead of making excuses and praising her son when he is wrong, she should let him know that his actions are affecting his children.

Mothers of the fathers of the fatherless children, you all have to be humble, discipline yourselves and respect the wishes of the mother of your grandchildren. Make it your personal mission to be in your grandchildren's lives, even if your son chose to take himself out of the equation.

Mothers of the fathers of the fatherless children, you are a mother, therefore, you should truly understand and be sincere regarding where the mother of your son's children is coming from. Not to mention, grandparents, you are not helping your son by making undercover moves. More so, you are hindering him from being a father, and you are helping him stray off track even further. As mothers, we have to work together for a far greater change than being biased and taking someone's side, especially knowing they are in the wrong.

Grandparents of the fathers of the fatherless children, clearly you are the observer of what is going on. There isn't a reason why you should be passive and/or stir up the pot and make matters worse. You should strive to ease the world of distractions and confusion without being biased, for your grandchildren's sake.

The blame game is very common when both parents can't agree to disagree. For some apparent reason, the fathers of the fatherless children think they have the right to run away when things don't work out in their favor.

Not only is the mother blamed for keeping the children away, but the children are also blamed if the fathers of the fatherless children do not like what they hear.

For the first time in a long time, Elijah saw his father when he was four years old. Five years had passed, and he decided he wanted to see Elijah when he was nine. He talked to him on the phone every now and then, but he didn't visit him for quite some time.

Elijah was happy to see his father, but he didn't get his hopes up because he knew what to expect. We met at the skating rink – he was late (shaking my head). Time went by and Elijah wanted to play games and get a little snack at the rink. His father told him he didn't have any money. He left to go to the bank (I didn't understand why he didn't bring any money. I mean, goodness, he hadn't seen his son in five years).

I guess he thought it was going to be like the last occasion when he saw Elijah when he was four years old. We meet at Monkey Joe's. I paid for Elijah's admission and socks. His father walked in and started playing with him, which I didn't mind because Elijah got to spend time with his father. However, afterward, we went out to eat. His father said he wasn't going to eat (I guess he thought he had to pay for me too). I ordered a meal for myself and Elijah; his father sat at the table with a glass of water and watched us eat. Naturally, I paid for my food, which wasn't a problem. However, his father didn't attempt to pay for Elijah's food, so, I paid for Elijah's food as well.

Nope, I wasn't going to deal with it this time around. I am a skater, so I went on the skating rink, minding my business while my daughter kept an eye on Elijah.

The next day, we meet at Sky Zone. My daughter and I sat in the front while Elijah and his dad played. This time around, I let him pay for Elijah's wristband and kept my distance. Afterward, we went to Red Robin to eat. Elijah's father said, "Red Robin is too expensive and I'm not hungry."

Elijah and his father sat at one table. My daughter and I sat at another. When the bill came, the waiter put all the meals together and gave me the tab. Ugh. I told her to take Elijah's father's food off (yes, he decided to eat this time around), and I would pay for Elijah's meal.

I guess he felt some kind of way because he said, "I will pay for Elijah's meal."

I asked him, "Are you sure?"

"Yes," he replied.

The next day, when Elijah's father arrived up north, Elijah had many questions for him. However, he hesitated to answer, but Elijah finally got an answer to one of the questions. Elijah asked his father, "Why did you leave me?"

"I had to take care of my mother," his father answered.

"That is not good enough!" Elijah said angrily.

"What do you mean, it's not good enough? You are being disrespectful," his father said. "I am not being disrespectful. I am angry! I am mad! You do not do anything for me. My mother takes care of me. You are never around," Elijah replied.

"I bought you some clothes and stuff. Why is that not good enough?" he answered.

"Forget the clothes. I would like you to be around more," Elijah told him.

The conversation didn't get far. Two months passed and Elijah's father didn't reach out. Elijah called him to tell him what he wanted for Christmas. He repeated it over and over again because his father kept saying, "What did you say?

Elijah said, "I want Beyblades. Repeat. I want Beyblades. My grandmother's address is… Repeat. My grandmother's address is…"

His father called me when he got off the phone with Elijah and said, "I do not know if you condone him disrespecting me. Saying repeat after he saying something is rude and disrespectful."

"How dare you even think I would allow Elijah to disrespect you? I am the one who's always preaching to him to always respect his father, whether you are in his life or not," I replied.

Our conversation turned into a huge argument. Needless to say, eight years and counting Elijah didn't get anything for Christmas or for his birthday (I must say, his father calls faithfully every year to tell Elijah happy birthday) from his father.

February, came around and it was Elijah's birthday. His father called for the first time since November.

"Elijah, your dad is calling. Do you want to speak to him?" I asked.

"No, Momma, I want to enjoy my birthday," he replied.

"Elijah, you should talk to him. At least he took the time out to call." I replied.

"Okay," he agreed.

"Hello," Elijah said as he answered.

"Hello. Happy Birthday," his father said.

"Thank you," Elijah replied.

What are you doing for your birthday?" he asked.

"My mom got me a birthday cake. I got what I wanted for my birthday.

Now I am going out to eat and celebrate my birthday with my family," he replied.

"That's good. Elijah, why haven't you called me?" his father asked.

"Because I didn't want to talk to you," Elijah answered.

"You know, I do not think that is fair," his father said.

"I do not think it is fair that you left me to help your mother," Elijah replied.

"That is disrespectful, Elijah," his father said.

"You know what? I am going to enjoy my birthday. I am not about to go through this again today. Goodbye," Elijah said as he hung up.

I corrected Elijah and told him he shouldn't ever hang up on his father. I went on to say, "I know he made you mad, but you shouldn't ever be disrespectful."

His father called back later, blaming Elijah for not calling him and not forming a relationship. I had to excuse myself from the restaurant, and I let him have a piece of my mind. I was not going to allow him to blame a ten-year-old little boy for his mess-ups. My son was a kid. A child. I told his father to man up or ship out. I told him to contact Elijah when he gets his shit together because we are not going to fall victim to his faults. I was so mad. My last words to him were "Own up to your shit; it's all or none. Pick one." I never understood Elijah's father motives. He always blamed everyone for what he extremely lacks. Sad to say, the last birthday party he attended, Elijah was three years old. Truth be told, fathers of the fatherless children, how dare you to play the victim when you never took your role as being a father seriously. Fathers of the fatherless children, you cannot expect to "receive if you never gave/give." Take responsibility for your actions.

Father of the fatherless children, how dare you blame a child for your wrong-doing? How dare you continue to blame the mother of your child? Correct yourself and own up to the mess you made in your life and your child's life. This is not your child's fault. They are innocent. You have nobody to blame but yourself. Either you are going to get on the bus or get left behind. Remember, one person doesn't stop the show, and life goes on whether you are in your child's life or not. It is your choice.

Whatever decision you make, know, it will be a decision you will have to live with for the rest of your life.

6

Missing Hero

Father of the fatherless son, you are like a thief in the night, because you robbed your son's peace. You have taken your son's innocence; a little boy should live the life of a little boy, full of love, light, happiness, and free will. Sadly, there are a lot of little boys in the world today, taking on your role to help support their mother put food on the table, pay bills, etc. You say to yourself, *I do not care* and *I do not want to know*. You should care. You should want to know; because that little boy is a part of you.

You son is growing up faster than he should. He is making "grown man" moves that are dangerous and a hazard to his life. Father of the fatherless son, you are nowhere to be found as your son slips into the deep end of destruction. Lend both of your hands, your heart, actions, and words to pull him up out of the deep end.

Father of the fatherless son, is it fair that your son has to lose himself, knowing you can help save him? Are you going to stand there and watch your son slip further and further into a path that will change his life forever?

Sadly, the path your son took started from your son silently crying for your presence, love, and attention.

Father of the fatherless son, your son is tired of being cut by you and bleeding to death as he tries to gain your attention. However, you do not see his suffering.

Father of the fatherless son, your son is tired of being pulled in two because of your careless selfish ways. However, you choose to isolate yourself and ignore your son's pain.

Father of the fatherless son, your son is walking down a path blindly, not knowing what is ahead—but you do; yet, you let him keep walking without warning. Your son is in too deep to get out of his own head, and trying to figure out what's next. Your son's eyes are wide open, but he doesn't see a thing. He is fighting unanswered questions deep inside that only you can answer, such as, why you do not want him? Why you do not love him? Why did you leave him? Why do you never want to see him? What has he done to deserve such treatment? Why is he's taking on your role as a man when he's only a little boy?

Father of the fatherless son, listen to your son's silent cry. Your son cannot escape because it is a concern that cannot be undone. The storm has traumatized his mind. While you are alive and well, you owe your son answers. Sadly, some fathers will not ever get a chance to talk to their son. There are little boys, young men, and grown men who will never receive an answer to their questions; they will always have deep wounds because their father is deceased and they have to make peace with the questions they will never have answers too.

The last time my oldest son saw his biological father, he was six years old, walking into a funeral home to view his body. He never had a connection with him. Maybe he would have had a connection if his father hadn't broken his promises.

The last time my oldest son saw his father alive, he was four years old. He came to his soccer game. My son had to have had about ten games and his father never made time to attend one. He promised my son he would show up on time to watch him play; instead, he showed up when the game was over. My son and I were walking hand-and-hand to our car. His father talked to him for about ten minutes and went on his way.

That wasn't the first time he had broken his promise. When my son was three years old, his father was supposed to meet my son and me at the park. My son had a yellow baseball bat and a humongous white ball as we waited and watched the cars pass by. My son saw a car that was similar to his biological father's. The car didn't slow down.

He said, "Mom why didn't he stop? He kept driving."

"It wasn't your father's car," I replied.

We waited and waited. He never showed up. My son was upset and threw his bat as far as he could. He ran into my arms as he cried out of hurt and from another disappointment. Afterward, we walked for a little while; he felt better after I played baseball with him, and later I took him to get some ice cream.

Throughout his life, he didn't have a father figure. My son had me. The Chief Guardian, of course. Not only was I his mother, but I was also his protector, and I played the missing hero as well.

I made a baby book for my children. I have pictures of my children from when they were in my belly until now. When my son was one year old, his father's family came to his birthday party, but his father wasn't there. Like always, he came when the event was over. He brought a red tricycle for my son. One of the best things he did was stay and put the tricycle together.

He was a "revolving door" father. He showed up at birthday parties, and sometimes at Christmas. The last birthday he attended was my son's third birthday. It was at an Early Learning Center. Again, I might add, he showed up when the party was over.

He didn't stop the show. As I look back at my oldest son's pictures, they bring me sweet joy as I look at him blowing out his candles, opening presents, and dancing. My son had a wonderful birthday – and that's what mattered the most.

When I met my ex-husband, he played the father role. He was a good father to my children, and I appreciated it greatly. He was very active in their lives. My oldest son was so comfortable with him, he asked him if he could call him Dad.

My ex-husband was in my son's life for five years; however, after he left me, he walked out of my oldest children's lives as well.

When my oldest son was ten years old, he told my ex-husband face-to-face that he did not ever want to be like him; and that he wouldn't walk out on his family. He said, "I knew you weren't my biological father, but I looked up to you as a father figure and I called you my dad. I was happy and proud to call you my dad, but you left me. You left all of us."

My oldest is a man, and growing, at twenty years old. I see that it is very imperative that a father partakes in his son's life. There were times when my son felt left out of place when my ex-husband left. Life was confusing because, unlike his friends, he didn't have a father in his life. He only had me as his mother growing up. I was the only parent there at his events.

Having a father makes a difference in a little boy's, a young man's, and a grown man's life. When my ex-husband was in my oldest son's life, I didn't have to carry the load as both a mother and father. I had the opportunity to step aside to let him raise him as a young boy. For a couple of years, he participated in parent-teacher conferences, we had family outings, and he was very active in my oldest son's extra-curricular activities. He was a good father to him.

However, when my oldest was in fourth grade, he left. That crushed my son, and I had to step up to the plate as before to be the Chief Guardian.

Fathers of the fatherless son's, wake up and see that your son needs you in his life. If you are involved in a child's life for years and he isn't your biological son, and you form a bond with him—it is not right for you to walk out of the little boy's life. That little boy formed a connection with you; as you did with him. That shouldn't be a bond that is easily destroyed or lost.

Fathers of the fatherless sons, your son has a heart. Your son has feelings. Fathers of the fatherless sons, your son's heart is hurting; he needs you in his life just as much as you need him in yours. He yearns for your love, dedication, support, and leadership.

Fathers of the fatherless sons, you shouldn't want the streets to raise your son. The streets do not love your son; they are using your son and making him a "do-boy" to do their dirty work. Man up, father of the fatherless sons. Believe it or not, your presence is needed. You are wanted and your presence is a "must-have." You can make a huge, significant difference in your son's life; his present and future. You have the ability to turn your son's life around for the better.

Fathers of the fatherless sons, you have the ability to hold and carry your son when he's an infant. You have the ability to teach your son right from wrong while he is a young boy, and in his teenage years. You have the ability to teach him what it is and what it is going to be like being a man. As he grows, every single day, you are forming your son to be the best man he can be.

After I gave birth to my youngest son my husband (at the time), cradled our son in his arms. It was a precious moment. It was amazing to see him hold his son. The way he looked at our son, I knew he wouldn't let any harm or pain shatter his life. Sadly, he was the one to inflict sadness and pain in our son's life. He left me to raise our son on my own when my son was five months old.

A couple of months passed and the next thing I knew, years had passed. Time doesn't wait on anyone. However, for some apparent reason, some people do not value time. They think time pauses and time waits for them. Wake-up call – time ticks by every nanosecond.

As my youngest son grew older and wiser, he knew he was missing out on his father. He would ask me. "Momma, where is my dad?" I told him he lives up north and he can call him if he likes. My son soon realized that his father didn't participate in his life. Elijah felt like the odd boy out. His classmate's fathers came to portfolios, morning meetings, and when they were performing. Everyone's father was at soccer games, and very active in their life.

One day, in fourth grade, Elijah, came home and said, "Momma, you know what one of my classmates asked me today?"

"What did he ask you?" I replied.

"He asked me where is my dad because they've never seen him before."

"Well, Elijah, what did you say?" I asked.

"I told him, I have one, but I don't call him Dad. I call him by his name, and he's up north with his mom. My momma is my mother and father."

There were times when Elijah asked his father questions that he didn't receive a direct answer to. His dad danced around the questions that were asked. There were many times when Elijah didn't want to talk to him because of the many broken promises he would make such as, telling Elijah he would get this or that for Christmas and never send anything. Or he would 'send' certain clothes or shoes for school and they never came in the mail. Elijah took what his father said and did at face value because it was a repeated cycle.

When Elijah was ten, he told his father how he felt; and his father didn't like what he heard. Honestly, I was glad that Elijah voiced his opinion and got it off his chest because I didn't want him to go on in life thinking he was at fault. I didn't want his father's distance to block his happiness and from living life.

Elijah's father and I have had many arguments because he felt that Elijah was disrespectful. I corrected Elijah. However, I voiced my opinion to his father and said, "It is only fair that Elijah tells you how he feels. He deserves to get his feelings off his chest. It isn't fair for a child in primary school to hold such a burden, heavy stress, and disturbing depression inside."

I told his father to man up and take the heat, for he caused this on himself. It never amazes me how people who know they are at fault never want to sit in the hot seat. It never surprises me how they never see their faults. Elijah's father really didn't and still does not until this day sees his mistakes. Like I told him, "Dude, you have to take the heat from the fire." I stated that he fails to realize Elijah is not the five-month-old he left; he is now ten years old. He is a wise young boy who understands the "part" he "chooses to play."

His father was very upset with Elijah because Elijah called him by his first name. His father was going back and forth with me saying, I made Elijah call him by his first name. That was never my doing. Whenever his father did call—eighty percent of the time I would say, Elijah, your dad is on the phone. There were times, I called him by his first name because he isn't my dad, therefore, I called him by his name.

Regardless of what I said, his father didn't understand. He would argue with Elijah and tell him, to call him Dad, not his given name.

Elijah, said to his dad, "You haven't been a Dad to me. You have never been in my life. You do not support me in school, my momma and my teachers do. You never come to any of my soccer games. My momma pays for me to play soccer, takes me to each practice and supports me at every game. You do not know what I like or dislike. You do not know what size shoes or clothes I wear. You do not know anything about me. You only know my name. Therefore, I will not call you my dad. I will call you by your name and your name only. If you cannot accept that, I do not have to call you anything, because I do not owe you anything."

Fathers of the fatherless sons, your sons want to give love and to be loved. You are the ones who choose not to give them a chance at getting to know and love you. When you all finally come around; most of the time it is too late. You've left your sons broken and bruised in so many ways. The fact of the matter is, fathers of the fatherless sons, you do not see the damage you have caused.

After Elijah's father was going back and forth with him, Elijah made the decision that he didn't want to talk to him anymore. His father blamed me, saying, "Charlena, you put this in his head." Little did he know, I used to make Elijah talk to him. When Elijah was younger, I made him get on the phone. When his father felt like calling, I had to bribe Elijah with something he liked so he would talk to him. Yet he said it was my doing when Elijah didn't want to talk to him. I was tired of being blamed.

As Elijah got older, he made a contract for me to sign. It stated, "My dad calls every three to six months, or when he feels guilty or just so happens to think of me. He thinks I'm supposed to talk to him when he feels like it. Momma, the contract states that you will not make me talk to him whenever he decides to call. Please ask me before you answer the phone if I want to talk to him or not. Momma, you cannot make me talk to him."

When I read that contract, I was taken aback because I never knew my son felt this way. I made him talk to his father when he called—because his father or his side of the family can't ever say I kept Elijah away from them. What hurt me the most was, I didn't know my making Elijah talk to him was hurting him. However, I do know if his father or his family say I kept Elijah away, Elijah can always say, no, when I didn't want to talk, my momma made me talk to you.

From that day forth, I never made Elijah talk to him. However, I did tell Elijah he could call his dad whenever he wanted to; all he had to do was ask. When Elijah's father decides to call—I will let Elijah know before I answer. However, Elijah would say, "Momma, I do not want to talk." I honor Elijah's wishes—and tell him to think about calling his father back. Sad to say, Elijah does not think anything of it—he would carry on with his day as if the conversation he and I had never existed.

Sadly, Elijah doesn't ask to call his father. Every now and then I'll say, "Elijah, I noticed your dad hasn't called in a while, do you want to call him?" He will say, "No, he can call me if he wants to."

Fathers of the fatherless sons, honestly, there's nothing you can say to defend yourself when your son tells you the truth. There is nowhere you can hide from all the madness that you've caused. Sadly, you will never take the blame for the mess you've made. Sooner or later, your selfish ways will be closing in and weighing very thin as the truth destroys your sense of peace.

Fathers of the fatherless sons, you need to recognize the mission your son is on; and it is bigger than themselves; you are the centerpiece. However, you cannot make up for the milestones you've missed. You can't be your son's hero when he's grown and has his own family and children.

Father of the fatherless son, you are your son's missing hero. Let it be known, you do not have the right to take offense when another man steps in and raises your son. If you are alive and well, it is a shame that another man has to step up to the plate to raise your son to be a better man than you. However, it is a lovely thing for your son, because blood doesn't always run deep. Love runs deep and love conquers all hearts, bodies, and souls.

Your son's 'father' who's raising him, cannot give him answers to your questions; however, he can give ("your") his son answers to the tough questions about life by living by example and putting in the time and work necessary to raise ("your") his son.

Father of the fatherless son, when you see your son doing well, know it is no thanks to you. It is because your son has his mother (the Chef Guardian) and his Hero in his life; his beloved father, who loved him, knowing his blood isn't running through ("your" son's) veins.

Father of the fatherless son, you should always be filled with gratitude that another man raised your son when you made the decision to walk away. As another man ("your" son's father) raised your son he instilled leadership abilities, unbelievable strength, unshakable survival skills, great respect for others, and helped your son find a purpose in life.

Father of the fatherless son, know you can be your son's protector, a healer, an inspiration, and a hero in your son's life instead of being the missing hero. You have the ability to empower your son to let him know he can and will do anything if he puts his mind to it; and as you lead by example.

Father of the fatherless son, do not underestimate the impact of your physical and emotional absence. Do not limit your role in your son's life. Be the tools your son needs to help build his present and future.

Father of the fatherless son, now is the time to take ownership and see your own responsibility in the problem. Do not be a missing mystery. Do not be a fatherless father that covers up his flaws. Own up to it, and be the start of healing the unhealed fatherless son.

7

Fatherly Fairy Tale

Daughters are precious little angels. They are delicate and pure. Little girls should always feel and know they are protected by their fathers.

A little girl should feel unconditional love from her daddy. Daddy's are the first love in a little girl's life. Daddy's are a little girl's hero, a Superman. He can do no wrong in his little girl's eyes because of the love he gives. No man can replace a daddy's love.

A little girl falls in love with her daddy because he loved her first. A daddy's love provides so much security, love, and support. A daddy's love makes a little girl feel like she can conquer the world as long as she knows her daddy is by her side and supports her every move.

Father of the fatherless little girl, where are you? What are you thinking? Do you know your little girl needs you more than ever when she is young, fragile, at times brittle, and so innocent? Your little girls need your comfort and your unconditional love. She needs to know you support her and will protect her with your life.

A daughter's first love should be her daddy. A daddy's presence comfort's the soul of a little girl. A daddy's love is so gentle, sensitive, and tender when it comes to his little girl. He is patient and willing to understand every moment and every step at any given time to make sure he crossed all his t's and dotted all his i's when it comes to his little girl. A daddy's love is a bond that will never be broken or forsaken in a little girl's, teenager's, and a grown woman's life. I am thirty-nine years old and I will always and forever be my daddy's little baby girl.

When I was a little girl, my daddy was Superman; I always thought my daddy could do anything and beat everybody up. I always use to tell people, "My daddy is strong and he will beat up the world if they try to hurt me." My daddy always made me felt protected and loved.

My daddy taught my sisters and me how to skate when we were around four years old, and every Saturday he would take us to Screaming Wheels. My daddy was very active in his daughter's lives.

My daddy was so patient with his daughters, and we couldn't do any wrong in his eyes. I knew we got on our daddy's nerves! God help his soul, he had three daughters, but he was never impatient with us. If he was—he never showed it.

When I lost my teddy bear (Nene), my daddy was the first person I told. He looked high and low to help me find it. He would look under the couch, in the kitchen cabinets, in the car, under the bed, and all over to find my teddy bear. He didn't stop looking for it until we found it.

If my siblings didn't want to play, he would stop what he was doing to play baby dolls with me. We would have a tea play-date as he sipped "pretend" tea from my little teacups. My daddy would put on an apron and bake a cake with my sisters and me with our Easy Bake Oven. Afterward, he would help clean the plastic dishes in our play kitchen. My daddy was amazing with his little girls.

I feel bad for little girls who don't have their daddy in their life because they are missing out on precious memories. My sisters and I used to do and say the darnedest things. My daddy used to say, "My babies made my day!"

When we colored outside the lines and thought our picture was ugly; my daddy used to put it on the refrigerator or in his office and say, "Are you kidding me? Are your eyes working? Do you see what I see?"

My sisters and I would say, "Yes, our eyes are working, Daddy? Yes, Daddy, we see what you see. Do you see what we see, Daddy?"

He would pick us up in his arms and say, "This is the best picture in the whole world." When he put us down he used to give us a sloppy wet kiss on the check. As we were about to wipe it off, he would say, "Do not wipe off my love!" So funny, my sisters and I walked around with wet cheeks until it dried up, careful and being mindful of what we did because we didn't want to wipe off Daddy's love.

My daddy used to always dance with my sisters and me! Whether we were standing on his toes as he led the way or if we were break dancing all over the place. My daddy favorite dance was the moonwalk. He was funny and took it so seriously—he would moonwalk in the kitchen, hallway, and living room. All of us would be in our socks sliding backward. He would pick us up one by one and spin us around and seal it with a wet kiss on our cheeks.

As I think about the memories when I was a little girl; it saddens me because my daughter will never have memories with her father. My daughter's father decided to distance himself after we broke up. My daughter was a couple of months at the time. There were times when his mother reached out and she spent time with Sarah, but that ended because she was always sneaky when it came to her son. I would tell her, it is okay for him to see Sarah at the house but please do not let him take Sarah anywhere. She never honored my wishes, therefore, I had to look out for my baby's safety.

Sarah's father had a drinking problem. His license was always suspended, and he always had warrants out for his arrest. He always had a lot of women in his life. Things were so bad, some of the women he was messing with thought we were still together and keyed my car. I drove around with the word 'bitch' on my car.

There were women harassing me and my daughter. Calling early in the morning after I dropped my daughter off at school, saying they were going to kidnap her. It got so bad, women would call me and ask me if I knew where he was. It was hell. Nearly every day, I had to let women know he and I were not together anymore. It was horrible. I had to move out of my apartment and changed my number for the safety of my children and myself. After I moved, I never heard from the women again.

Father of the fatherless daughter, how do you think you can raise a daughter constantly being in and out of jail because of your own careless reasons? Why would you want all kinds of different women around your daughter? What kind of picture do you think you are painting? You are painting a picture of poor performance of what a father and/or man should be in your daughter's life. More than likely, your daughter is going to find a man just like you. Do you want that for your daughter? Father of the fatherless daughter, you should want to live by example; therefore, as your little girl grows, she would know her worth and how she should be treated as a woman.

My daughter's father has never been to her birthday party a day in his life. The first and last time my daughter remembering seeing her biological father she was six years old. My husband at the present time was her father; he was the only father my daughter had known since she was eighteen months old.

When we met up with her biological father, his mother, wife, and children were there. Things were kind of odd. Her biological father was happy to see her and he smiled from ear to ear, as he said, "Oh my goodness, look, she has my toes!"

His mother was happy to see her too, as she asked tons of questions, trying to get to know her granddaughter. Sarah held on tight to her Dad (who was my husband at the time). He made her feel safe and protected.

As hours had passed, we went outside to take pictures. Sarah's biological father's wife said, "Sarah, you want to take a picture? Go stand over there near your daddy?" Sarah, ran over to her dad, smiling as she posed for the picture to be taken.

His wife said, "No, stand over there with your real daddy."

That was disrespectful, and she should have known better to say that to a little child who was seeing her biological father for the first time ever.

I corrected her and said, "Sarah's daddy is standing right over there, the man who is my husband, who's been Sarah's father since she was nearly two years old. Do not ever disrespect him or my family ever again. Most importantly, do you not think you confused my daughter? Shame on you."

As we prepared ourselves to go, we felt bombarded, as his mother had a list of people she wanted Sarah to see. She said, "If you do not mind, may I take Sarah to see my mother, my sisters, her cousins, etc."

I didn't have a problem with that. However, I made it known, I would be there.

We spend time with his mother every now and then without her biological father. After a short time passed, she wanted to have Sarah alone. However, Sarah wasn't comfortable. I explained to her that Sarah wasn't ready. That is when one of the issues began.

I tried to make plans over and over again to meet up with Sarah's biological father, his wife, and Sarah's sisters, however, it wasn't successful. Sarah knew of her oldest sister and they used her as bait. When Sarah called to talk to her, they would say she wasn't home or make up an excuse for Sarah to talk to her youngest sister. Needless, to say Sarah never talked to her oldest sister. What made matters worse, his wife called me saying things had changed since Sarah came into their lives. She said, "Sarah, is getting all of the attention and my children aren't getting attention from their grandmother. You all just came in and took over."

Filled with anger, she said, "By the way, you do not want Sarah to come over here alone with my husband, because he is still a drunk. I do not trust him around my children alone."

I didn't know if she was lying or telling the truth. However, I spoke with him, and apparently, that caused confrontation between them. She threatened to take me to court for custody (when they had only seen Sarah one time). We went back and forth arguing. I wasn't going to entertain her any longer, so I stopped all communication. I knew my daughter wouldn't be in a healthy environment and my daughter's safety was my priority.

I hate that my daughter never had a relationship with her biological father. She is now seventeen years old; with the hope that one day she will be able to talk to him without interference from others.

I, as the Chef Guardian, have been both mother and father to my daughter. My sweet little girl has always gotten the shitty end of both sticks when it came to having a father in her life. Most of the time, I blame myself for the people I've chosen.

Sadly, when my daughter was eight years old my ex-husband told my daughter he wasn't her father; he is only Elijah's father. My daughter was beyond hurt; she was devastated and very disappointed. She changed, and she started to not trust any man. My ex-husband was the only father she known, and for him to out of the blue one day crush her spirit, was a game-changer.

I never made it difficult for him to see the children. So I never understood how he could coldly make that decision and tell a little girl who only knew him and him only as a father, that no, he cannot be her dad. How selfish was that? That was low down, dirty, and cutthroat.

Fathers of the fatherless daughters, if you've invested great time and years into a child's life; you are considered one way or another to be a father figure in that child's life. Before you step into a child's life who isn't biologically yours, think before you take charge and move forward.

Fathers of the fatherless little princesses, there shouldn't be anything you wouldn't do for your little girls to make them happy. You should want to move heaven and earth for your daughters, even if it takes every breath of your body. Every night, you should fall asleep knowing you've done all you could do every single hour for your baby girl.

I had a beautiful white cat named Pammie. I loved her so much! When I was seven years old, she was run over by a car. Everyone knew how much I loved my Pammie. A next-door neighbor knocked on our door telling us the news. I ran in my parent's room, screaming at the top of my lungs, saying, "Daddy! Daddy! Daddy! Pammie got hit by a car! Help her, Daddy, please, help her!"

My daddy said, "It's going to be okay." He ran outside, picked Pammie up, made a bed for her in a cardboard box, and took her to the vet. Every day, Daddy went up to the vet and checked on Pammie. When he brought Pammie home, she had lost one eye, and her legs were broken. I loved Pammie back to good health. However, months later Pammie wandered away. I think she went away to die. I was so hurt. I wouldn't eat, couldn't sleep, and I didn't want to play with anyone.

My daddy came home early one afternoon and said, "I have a surprise for you!" I looked at him and really didn't care what the surprise was. I looked in the box, and he had adopted a cat from the Atlanta Humane Society. Although it wasn't Pammie, I was so hurt and happy at the same time.

My daddy loved me so much, he took time out to rush my cat to the veterinarian and got me another cat after Pammie wandered away. That meant a lot to me because my feelings mattered to my daddy. The love he had for me spoke louder than words.

Fathers of the fatherless daughters, you sweet little precious girls should be your lifeline; they are filled with so much love and hope when it comes to their father. If a father is in his little girl's life, she will be quick to talk to you first before anyone else. She will trust you to tell you all of her thoughts because she knows you will tell her the truth in the most heartfelt way.

After my husband left me. My daddy stayed on the phone listening to me sob for hours. There were times when I didn't say anything at all. He would say, "Baby girl, are you there?" As I started to cry again and said, "Yes, I am here." Him asking me, "Are you there?" meant a lot to me, because my daddy took the time to listen and held the phone until I was ready to get off.

Fathers of the fatherless daughters, little things, such as holding the phone, matter. Little things, such as listening, means a lot. Little things, such as giving your daughter a hug shows her you love her. Things such as giving advice are such a huge step because your daughter will know she can always talk to you about anything.

Father of the fatherless daughter, there is no man who can fill the void of not having a father in her life. Not having a father in her life causes "daddy issues" such as not being able to trust a man. Looking for a man/boyfriend to be her father. Your daughter will be terrified of a man's love. She will always feel like a man will always neglect her; even if a good man comes into her life.

Father of the fatherless daughter, you are setting your daughter up for failure. You are showing your daughter there is no such thing as true love and happiness. Father of the fatherless daughter, do you not think your daughter deserves your love? Do you not think when she's older she deserves to be truly loved and to know what love should be from a man?

My daddy is my first love; he taught my sisters and me how a woman should be treated. Growing up, he taught us how to think like a man and act like a lady at all times; because men take advantage of women who they think are weak-minded.

It is your responsibility as a father to show her; her worthiness of what love can really be.

When I went on my first date, my daddy grilled my boyfriend. I was so embarrassed and mad at the same time. After my date dropped me off, the next day, he broke up with me and told everybody my daddy was crazy. I was so mad at my daddy, but I knew my daddy had my best interests at heart. He was protecting me and wanted to make sure I was in good hands. Months passed, my date and I became a couple. As the years passed, my daddy, got to know him and accepted our relationship. I must say, it wasn't easy for my boyfriend, but he knew the rules and regulations. He treated me with the utmost respect because he knew my daddy didn't play.

Father of the fatherless daughter, you too should be there for each and every one of your daughter's dates. You should scope him out and let your daughter know if he's a good man or to get rid of him. Father of the fatherless daughter, you are shaping your daughter's present and future; for they put all of their trust in you. Give your little girl the opportunity to form a bond with you; to trust you, and to be her Superman when she needs a hero.

Father of the fatherless daughter, your little girl is beautiful. You should be willing to provide your male energy of self-worth, self-love, self-confidence, strength, and courage to your daughter. Trust me when I say, she will feel like she is on top of the world!

My daddy taught us to always speak our mind in a respectful way. He was strict, yet humble. My daddy is a Marine; therefore, we had a lot of rules and regulations in our household. As I am now older, I appreciate the rules and regulations, because it made me who I am today. A strong lady; who knows not to take no for answer; and to stand up for what I want and believe in. My daddy is an amazing man, and I am blessed every single day, that he is my daddy.

My daddy always took up for his girls. When the teacher would say we did this or said that my daddy used to ask the teachers, "Well, what did you say to my daughter?" The teacher would say, "It doesn't matter what I said. Your daughter needs to give me respect." My daddy would say calmly, "With all due respect, I teach my children that to receive respect you must earn respect, regardless of age, color, gender, etc. I ask again, what did you say to my daughter?" The teacher admitted her error. However, father of the fatherless daughter, you are the one who gives your little girls that drive to want to do better; to stand up for her rights and what she believes in. You are the one who gives your daughter the courage to conquer her dreams. By her knowing you are there for her, you give her unbelievable powers that she has never known.

Father of the fatherless daughter, you cannot be upset if another man raises your little girl. If he brought her up to be the woman she is; you need to thank him for doing your job. I have several students who, as females, were raised by another man. Who they call their daddy, who they love so dearly. I've heard stories about when their biological father wanted to come back into their lives, but my students said, they only needed three questions to be answered:

1. Why did you leave?
2. Where were you?
3. Did you ever think of me?

Some of my students received an answer that they accepted but moved on with their life without communicating with their fathers. Some of them never got an answer.

Father of the fatherless daughters, do not let your daughter's life pass you by. A daughter's love is so precious; you will never have to prove your love to her because she will accept you as you are. Do not be the reason why your daughter settles for a man for the wrong reasons. Do not be the reason why your daughter's self-esteem is shot down to the lowest level. Do not be the reason why your daughter's in a physical, verbal, and emotional abused relationship.

Father of the fatherless daughter, do not be the lost soul in your daughter's life. Play a major role in your daughter's life. She should always be her daddy's little princess, even when she is old and gray. She deserves to be happy! She deserves to be loved! She deserves joy! And she deserves you!

8

Blueprint

Our sons and daughters are a reflection of us. When they look in the mirror, they see features of their mother and father. Sadly, most of the time the only reflection they can compare and recognize is their mother. As our sons and daughters dissect the other half of themselves, they do not know where to start because the other half of their dimension is either never around or acts as a revolving door that is never stable.

Fathers of the fatherless sons and daughters, believe it or not, your children are curious. At a young age; that is when your sons and daughters are brighter than a billion stars in the sky. They are fearless as they ask a million-and-one questions, such as," Mommy, if I do not look like you, who do I look like? Mommy, why my eyes are different from yours? Mommy, why are my fingers long and yours short? Mommy, why is my hair curly and yours straight? Mommy, why am I lighter-skinned than you?" And the questions go on and on—and never-ending.

As they grow older, they become wise and realize a lot of things are not adding up; and their curiosity is taken up a notch. They notice things don't seem to be as they appear as their reality becomes perfect vision. Their ears filter the stories that once made sense when they were young, but now as they are older the stories are not lining up. They begin to see they were told too many lies from their mother and father. Our children begin to put the puzzle pieces together one by one.

Therefore, the hard questions are being asked as the Chief Guardian is unfairly backed into a corner. As mothers, we do not want to hurt our son's and daughter's feelings. We try to be mindful of how we answer tough questions they deserve to know the answers to. We have to make a cautious decision about whether to tell little white lies or tell the truth. Instead, we sugar-coat the fathers of the fatherless children's absence by covering up the truth with sweet white lies. As our sons and daughter ask, "Why didn't my daddy show up?"

Most of the time, the Chief Guardians will say, "He had to work late," or, "He had an emergency, he will stop by another time."

Sadly, "another time" came and went, and the fathers of the fatherless children never once showed up.

Fathers of the fatherless sons and daughters, it is awful how we as mothers have to argue or ask you consistently to spend time and help support your children. However, you all go around saying, "I do not spend time with my son or daughter because of his/her mother; she gets on my nerves. All she does is complain, fuss, and want to argue over nothing."

Correction! Reality check, fathers of the fatherless children. We, as the Chief Guardians, do not have time to argue with you. We are on a mission, trying to keep everything together for the sake of your children that you neglect to take care of. Instead of our sons and daughters having Superman in their life; they have a Superwoman in their life; fighting to make sure they eat, have clothes on their back, shoes on their feet, making sure they are healthy and well, we make sure they are getting a great education, providing for the things they need for school and working hard to make sure they have everything they need, etc.

Not to mention, our sons and daughters have dentist and doctor appointments quarterly; and God forbid if they become sick; we have to juggle that as we try to make it home before the sun from working two different shifts. Not only do we work two full-time shifts, but mothering our children is a full-time job in itself.

Fathers of the fatherless sons and daughters, the Chief Guardians you complain about are your son's and daughter's number one fans. Although our plates are running over, we still manage to make sure they are in extra-curricular activities to keep them busy. Fathers of the fatherless children, you better believe it, we, the Chief Guardians, are at every practice, every game, and every single performance. We, as Chief Guardians, show up and show out! We do what we have to do for our sons and daughters to survive.

Fathers of the fatherless children, you all complain about the Chief Guardians arguing or fussing to the point you do not want to put up with us. We fuss and argue with you because we go through so much raising your children alone. We argue with you because your children ask about you, and we are tired of making up lie after lie to make you look like Father of the Year.

Fathers of the fatherless son and daughters, your children want to see you, your children want to spend time with you, your children want you to be a part of their lives. You all are too focused on what you "think" you should be doing to benefit the mother. Let it be known, you are not doing the mother of your children any favors. The mother of your children is the one who is pulling the entire ship; it would be nice if you all jump on board to share the load.

Listen up, fathers of the fatherless sons and daughters, if our children didn't ask about you, we wouldn't waste our time calling you and pushing you to spend time and help support your children. It is a shame we have to ask. Honestly, asking you all to spend time with your children shouldn't be on the mother's agenda. It shouldn't be a thought that comes into your children's mind. It should be a given.

Fathers of the fatherless sons and daughters, your spitefulness isn't hurting the Chief Guardians. Your bitter ways are hurting your flesh and blood – your sons and daughters. Your deceptions are the dimensions of you. Your sons and daughters are a blueprint of you in so many ways, such as their height, features at every angle, physical appearance, size, and at times, the version of their character and attitude.

Fathers of the fatherless sons and daughters, you failed to realize your children are a blueprint of you. However, you are all so selfish you do not see your blueprint, the blueprint that you've created. You are put here to help and show them the way. You are the one who's supposed to layout the design plan for your sons and daughters.

Your design should teach your little boy the fundamentals of life. As he sprouts into a young man, you as his blueprint (father) should be more than willing to lead the way as you teach him how to make wise decisions as a young boy growing to be a mature man. There are so many things your son needs to know. He needs to know how to survive in this world. As he learns how to survive, then he will know how to live his life fearlessly.

Fathers of the fatherless sons, your sons are trying their best to find their way in life. Some of them are trying to do the best they can, but the streets are swallowing them whole. They do not know who to trust, and there are pretenders in the world acting as though they have your son's best interest at heart. They are only stripping your son of his identity, dignity, and willingness to change for the better. Fathers of the fatherless sons, you can save your son's life. Take hold of your responsibility and make a change.

Fathers of the fatherless sons, your son needs to know how it feels like to be loved, therefore, he would know how to love. As his blueprint, you should be teaching him how to be a family man as well. He needs to know how he should treat a woman, and how to take care of his family. However, with you being his blueprint you are an expert at showing him how to give up on life. He will be an expert on making babies and leaving them. Fathers of the fatherless son, your son's bad habits are many thanks to you. By your presence being missing in action in his life, he can't help but follow your blueprint of abandonment.

As Chief Guardians, it is hard raising our sons. It is very stressful because we are not men, we are women. We can only do what we think is best, and the best we can. My oldest son was hanging around the wrong crowd as he tried to impress his friends by borrowing other people's clothes. He wanted to fit in by having a phone; which I told him he could not have. However, he wanted a phone so badly to the point he was bold enough to take my friend's phone.

As Chief Guardian, I talked to him and laid down what I wasn't going to tolerate. He didn't pay me any attention until I had to show him that I am not a force to be played with. I told him to walk home. Instead, he called a family member who only shows up when drama appears. She took him to her house as she listened to the lies he told on me. What pissed me off the most, some of my family members were telling him that what he was doing was okay. My brother talked to my son and told him he needed to stop lying about his mother. He also told my son that I, as his mother, told him the right thing and that he needed to go home.

Long story short, while he thought he was making me look bad, he didn't get anything out of speaking badly about me. As he resided at my sister's place he wasn't fed or clothed, and he had to find his own way to school. After a week passed, I transferred him to another school. I talked to him and told him, as his mother, I only wanted what was best for him, and I work too hard for him to run the streets. I explained to him, the street was going to take his soul, and he was either going to be dead or in jail. After I transferred him into another school, he made friends that were on track and accomplishing their goals. He played tennis and was in the Early College Program.

As time went by, I had to talk to my son about sex. When he told me he was having sex, as Chief Guardian, I bought him condoms. I also bought him a baby doll, and I made him pretend that was his baby. During the week, I woke his butt up every three hours, he had to change and feed the baby. I took the baby doll to his tennis practice; he had to stroll it around in a stroller, change and feed the baby. His coach told him, "Please tell your mom you need to practice, we need to focus." I told my son, "Okay, get in the car and let's go home because your baby comes first." I explained to him when we got home that if he has children, they will be his priority, he will have to take responsibility, and his life will not be about him.

I am my son's blueprint. I lead by example. I made sure I kept a hold on him to the point he was in activities and staying out of trouble. If he decided to hang around the wrong crowd, I nipped that in the bud and found another option. I talked to him about the reality of life; because life is cutthroat, bittersweet, and filled with temptations. I refused to let my son be a product of the system. I was willing to make sacrifices to keep him on the right track. I do not regret giving up so much, turning down high-paying jobs that would not allow me to raise my son to be a man. I refused to let the streets raise him; therefore, every sacrifice I made was worth it; and I would do it again if I had to.

Fathers of the fatherless sons, you should want your sons to be better men than you. You should want to give them your all and your last. Step up, and be a man to your sons. You are their blueprint.

Our sweet little girls are beautiful and precious. They are so sensitive and innocent. They are little flowers that are blooming. As a little girl, I loved saying, Daddy! Daddy! Daddy! Knowing that I had a daddy made me feel so loved and wanted. Sadly, there are little girls in the world who would never call their fathers "Daddy." There are little girls walking this earth who don't know how and what it means to really say the word, "Daddy."

Fathers of the fatherless little girls, you have robbed your little girls from saying the loving powerful word, "Daddy." Fathers of the fatherless little girls, your little sunshine would never get the opportunity to call your name, "Daddy" as she runs into your arms, giving you a hug as she squeezes you so tight saying with such joy and excitement, "Hey, Daddy!" Father of the fatherless little sweet girls, how dare you take that right and those moments from your precious daughter?

One of the most precious moments, I had with my daddy was when my little brother was born. Everybody was telling me that I wasn't going to be the baby anymore. I was six years old when I looked at my little brother when he was a couple of hours old. All I could hear over and over again was people teasing me, saying, "You're not the baby anymore." I ran into my daddy's arms and cried. He carried me into the elevator and asked me, "Why are you crying?" I was crying so hard I couldn't catch my breath, "Because I am not the baby anymore," I answered, trying to wipe the tears off my face. My daddy looked at me, wiped my tears and said, "You will always be my baby girl." As I was in my daddy's arms, I laid my head on his shoulder because I knew I was always and forever going to be my daddy's little baby girl.

Fathers of the fatherless daughters, your sweet flowers need nurturing and to be taken care of. Little girl's hearts are so gentle and very sensitive.

You are supposed to be the one who puts her broken little heart back together when her favorite baby doll's arm is broken. When her best friend doesn't want to be her friend anymore, you should be the one playing dress-up with her. When your little girl grows, and her heart is broken for the first time by a young boy, you should be the one who mends her heart.

When my daughter was in kindergarten, my husband at the time was a work in progress as he fixed my daughter's hair. I thought it was the cutest thing when he had her bows in his mouth trying to twist or braid her hair. When she went to school; her teachers would ask, "Sarah, who did your hair today?" She would say, "My daddy."

As time went by, he became a pro! Her teachers were confused about whether I did her hair or my husband did.

Father of the fatherless daughter, small and cute little moments such as fixing your daughter's hair is a memory she will always remember.

Fathers of the fatherless daughters, your time is precious. Your time is wanted. Your time is needed in your daughter's life. You are the source and the definition of what a man should be in her life. Believe it or not, you help shape your daughter's character. She needs your guidance.

I am bold because of my daddy. I am insightful because of my daddy. I make sure I am respected by a man because my daddy made it known to my sisters and me; if a man does not respect you; you need to leave him be. My daddy always told my sisters and me; he wasn't always the best man to my mother, but as for his daughters he told us if a man cheats on you once; let him go. If you take him back; you are giving him permission to do it again. He raised the point that, if you are in a relationship and it doesn't work out; do not go back, keep moving forward after you gave it your all; There shouldn't be any should have, could have, or would have. If you tried and it didn't work; it didn't work out for a reason.

My daddy always taught his girls to speak our mind, because we have a voice; and to always remember our voice should always be heard, no matter what.

My daddy is my hero because he made sure another man didn't raise his girls.

When I needed to talk to my daddy, he was always there. No matter how long I talked; he sat, on the phone or face-to-face, and listened. My daddy always gave my sisters and me the best advice. He was always so patient with his girls. I'm sure I can speak for my sisters and myself when I say, our daddy is the best daddy in the Universe! He has done for much for us; his presence alone spoke a lot of volumes. There is no one else like our daddy, he means the world to us; and he is our hero forever and always.

Fathers of the fatherless daughters, when you are not in your daughter's life, they are wounded. If a young girl doesn't have a bond with her daddy that deeply affects her in multiple areas in life, such as physically, emotionally, and mentally. They are broken and bruised in so many ways because they are missing so much of you in their life. Their emotions are impacted because of your absence, they become involved in unhealthy relationships, and this triggers unresolved "daddy issues."

Father of the fatherless daughter, why would you want your daughter to be in a bad relationship because she doesn't know what a good man is? She missed out on learning what a good man could be because you weren't in her life. Why would you want your daughter to be in an abusive relationship because she thinks "getting hit" is "love?" She's so used to hearing the word "sorry" to the point she mistakes it for "I love you." Why would you want your daughter to walk the streets searching for love from a man when you should be the first man who loved her, and you should be the first man she ever loved. Father of the fatherless daughter, your little girl yearns for your love. Do not selfishly steal your love from your little girl.

My sister and her boyfriend got into a huge argument. My daddy was cutting the grass. Next thing I knew, my daddy walked to his truck and got out his pistol. He was marching to my sister's boyfriend's car. He broke his driver's side window with his gun, put it towards his head and said, "If you yell at my daughter one more time, I am going to shoot your fucking brain out! You better think twice before putting your hands on her or your mother going to be buying a black dress."

We knew our daddy would protect us at any cause. My daddy didn't play about a man yelling at his girls or making his girls cry. We are our daddy's heart, and forever and always will be.

Father of the fatherless daughter, your baby girl faces a lot of struggles and challenges by you not being there in her life. As she gets older, there are so many men who will deceive her; however, she wants to love and to be loved so badly she wouldn't be able to tell the difference. Father of the fatherless daughter, love your little sunshine; do not let her grow up feeling like she has to stay in a dysfunctional relationship because she fears being abandoned again. Also, do not let your daughter isolate herself because she is afraid of love. Your daughter is your blueprint, give her the love she deserves. Show her what love is, and give her the knowledge by your words and actions of what a good man is.

Fathers of the fatherless children, open the conversation, walk and stay in your children's lives. You can eliminate most of their bad choices such as substance abuse, depression, feeling lost, anxious about not feeling loved or wanted, etc. Heal your children's hearts, be your children's happiness, heal their journey because sooner rather than later you are not going to be able to fix what cannot be undone.

Fathers of the fatherless son and daughters, whether you are in your children's life or not, they are your blueprints and images of you walking the earth. Do not miss out, because some of them are moving forward without you. They are making a huge impact on the world, and they will make their mothers proud. It would be an honor if you would be a part of your blueprint's life and be a part of the legacy you've created, and this will continue from generation to generation.

I am proud to be a part of my daddy's blueprint!

I am more than sure that your children would love to be proud to have your blueprint and leadership in their life. Fathers of the fatherless children, your sons and daughters would love to know they are loved, protected, supported, and secured by you.

When all is said and done, fathers of the fatherless children, when your sons and daughters have moved on in their lives; accomplished their dreams without a light from your path, you have no right to be angry, bitter or upset. If you are, then you need to examine the man in the mirror. When you point one finger; you will have three fingers pointing right back at you.

Fathers of the fatherless children, whether you are in your son's and daughter's lives or not, they will be okay, they will make it somehow and some way without you. However, there will be some that will fall through the cracks by not having your present in their lives.

Fathers of the fatherless sons and daughters, as you let your sons and daughters fall through the cracks, it never fails that your children or the Chief Guardian see you out and about, shopping and taking care of someone else's children. How do you call yourself a man, knowing you are taking care of someone else's children and not your own? How do you think that makes your children feel? What makes matters worse, you all only pay the minimum in child support or nothing at all. There's no such thing as making time for someone else's child than your own. Fathers of the fatherless children, you need to seriously get your act together. If you are going to participate in another child's life, make sure you take care of your own flesh and blood first. Shame on you. Shame on you.

Chief Guardians work so hard to provide for our children because we want nothing but the best for our sons and daughters, as you should too. Chief Guardians always give our everything and the little fuel we have left without asking for anything in return. What saddens me, fathers of the fatherless children is that most of the Chief Guardians are on government assistance because they do not have the help they deserve from you. Are you comfortable with the government taking care of your children? Chief Guardians sacrifice so much for our children. We sacrifice so much because our babies are our blueprint, they are an image of us.

We are their leaders, role models, and our actions speak louder than our words. There are so many Chief Guardians who are barely getting by, but we make it happen; because our sons and daughters mean the world to us and we want them to have more than what we ever had. We want our children to have a happy, joyful, and fulfilled life.

Chief Guardians work so hard because we want our children to reap our benefits. We will work long and hard until the last piece of skin on our bones for them to have a great education and scholarships to go to school.

We give up our entire lives for our sons and daughters to have the best the world has to offer. At times, Chief Guardian's hard work goes unappreciated, but we keep making moves because we are thinking of the bigger picture. We want what's best for our children.

As our sons grow into men; we teach our sons *not* to be like you. They know they are loved, wanted, handsome, and supported. We raise them to respect women and to get an education. Some will make us proud, and some will disappoint; however, as Chief Guardians, we can sleep at night and say that for eighteen years, we did the best we could do alone.

As little girls grow into women, we, as Chief Guardians teach them *not* to be like you. We school them to not make the same mistakes we made in choosing the wrong men. We raised our daughters to know they are queens and to not accept anything less than that. Our daughters know, they are loved, beautiful, wanted and supported. Our daughters know they can do whatever they set their minds to do.

Fathers of the fatherless sons and daughters, remember, your children cannot eat excuses for dinner; "I'm sorry" doesn't cut it and is not accepted anymore. You have a choice to be authentic (real) or continue, as a synthetic, faded memory; and for some of you, you all can choose to be a "sperm donor." Take your pick, the choice is yours. Life goes on, and your sons and daughters will be loved and cared for by the Chief Guardians because we love our children more than life itself.

9

I Want You to Know

Fatherless children suffer from not having a father in their life. There comes a time when they have to accept their father's absence or let their father's absence steal their birthright of happiness and joy.

When our children think they are alone at a crossroad; the Chief Guardians are always there to lend a helping hand. As our fatherless sons and daughters prepare to cross over to claim their life purpose; they hesitate because they feel as though they are leaving an unknown part of themselves behind that will never be revealed.

Crossing over and leaving answers behind is difficult. Before this day, they had always felt helpless and hopeless because of abandonment and isolation.

Fathers of the fatherless sons and daughters; the time has come, and the time is now! This is the beginning for your children to take the first step to relieve their hurt and leave it behind. With each step, they are taking they are becoming one with themselves as they are done believing in your lies.

As they walk closer and closer peace is within and around them. They begin to think of the times they reached out to you for comfort and answers; however, they never felt the warmth from your love; instead, all they felt was the coldness from your heart.

Due to your absence, they do not know where they belong, but they are clearing their mind of doubt, stress, feeling unwanted, and unloved. As they cried tears of pain and hurt, they finally released the resentment; and now know what it feels like to truly smile.

As they think about how they tried over and over again to get your attention, your sons and daughters are using the DNA you gave them to form a new identity of their own.

Fathers of the fatherless children, as they have one foot in the past and one foot in their future, your sons and daughter are smiling as they release the pain you caused, and saying, "I am more than what you made of me. You might not think enough of me to see that I am someone special and unique. You cannot push or bully me around anymore because your thoughts don't matter. I gave you so much – and a part of me that you didn't deserve. This is the beginning of my new life. I am stepping out of a dream that is now a reality. It feels good to truly smile and feel anew. I am going to find my own way without you, and I want you to know; I am going to be okay."

Fathers of the fatherless sons and daughters, your children have crossed over to a life of letting go of the baggage that is not theirs to carry and the answers to their questions that they never received. They never heard you say. "I love you." They never got a heartfelt hug from you, and they never got to look at you in the eyes. They have awakened and achieved a balance of love, hope, peace, and happiness.

Your sons and daughters are free from your careless heart-stabbing and acts of spite and bitterness. Fathers of the fatherless children, you no longer have power over your children's minds, thoughts, emotions, and the appearance of stress which was written all over their faces. They have broken away and unleashed themselves from the chains.

They are flying, free as a bird! Look at them soar!

As they spread their wings and fly, their stress is released because they now know why they are here; they know that they are alive. They are here and alive to live a passionate, laughter-filled, happy, loving, fulfilled life of purpose, and peace. Fathers of the fatherless children, your wish is granted; you are completely cut out of the picture. Are you happy?

~ ~ ~

"Dear Invisible Father,

I have released the past of not having a father in my life. It took a toll on me; however, I am now forty years old. I sometimes wondered what I missed out on by not having you in my life, but I am now the father of three boys and one girl. They never have to worry about missing out on my undivided love. Dear Invisible father, I am happy to say I did not follow in your footsteps. I take pride in being a father. I want you to know that my bundles of joy are my life, my world; and I enjoy every second and every minute of the day I spend with them. Sadly, your loss, but my gain." ~Todd

~ ~ ~

"Dear Long-lost Father,

I am now sixteen years old. Where have you been? Are you alive? Are you well? When I look in the mirror, I wonder at times is yours the reflection looking back at me? Mother told me you had a DNA test. It came back 99.9% positive that my blood is yours. Did you get the result? Why did you never call me? I want answers. Why do you constantly ignore me? What did I do wrong? I need you in my life. I want you in my life. I know you do not want to be found. I am not going to stop searching. Lost father, I know you do not want to see me; but can you at least tell me where you are going to be? I won't bother you. Tell me what you are going to wear. I would be so happy if I could see you in passing. I promise I will not follow you. I want to see your face. As you walk away; I want you to know, I will keep my eyes on you as you fade into the background." ~ April

~ ~ ~

"Dear Stranger,

Although you do not have a clue, today is my birthday. I am twenty-one years old. I am officially legal. How is life treating you? I would like to know, do I have any sisters or brothers? Because of you, I ask every guy I date if they do not mind taking a DNA test. Since I never met you and I do not know if I have any siblings, I do not want to date my brother. They think I am crazy, I tell them my unknown father made me this way. I hope you are living the best life, that life has to offer. As for me, I want you to know that because of you, I live in a deep state of depression. Because of you, I push people away because I do not trust easily. Stranger, you are the weed in my life I try to cut every day. Sooner or later, I will mow the grass and treat the weed problem. I want you to know, I haven't got that far, because I linger on in hope." ~ Beth

~ ~ ~

"~Dear Missing in Action,

I am a brokenhearted son. My scars run deep. Most days I wonder, will I be like you? It bothers me because I wonder why do I think about someone I do not know. I can never put a face to a name. Your absence damaged my life. I finally know how to tie a tie – no thanks to you – all thanks go to YouTube. I had my first date last week, my momma, reminded me to greet my date with a smile, compliment her beauty, and open the door for her. Funny, I didn't have enough money, but Momma gave me what little she had to make sure my date and I had a good time. I want you to know, I am going to be a better man than you; maybe you can look up to me one day and take note." ~ Aaron

~ ~ ~

"Dear Deadbeat Dad,

It hurts that I am not on your love list. I never asked for much; the only thing I want is your love. You think that since I am eleven years old, I do not understand. I know you do not want me. The least you can do is be honest and tell me. Do you know what one of my classmates asked me today? He asked me, do I have a dad? I said, "Doesn't everyone have a father? I would think so." "Oh, I apologize. Did your father die?" he asked. "No, he's just a deadbeat," I replied. "Deadbeat, what is that? he asked. "He comes every around when he feels like it," I said. "Oh, that's great! I'm sure he comes around every day," he replied. "No, I am not on his love list." Deadbeat dad, I want you to know, I am on my mother's love list, and I am going to be an amazing son; you just watch and see." ~ Josh

~ ~ ~

"Dear Lost Love,

I have two younger sisters. Their father is my father too, I love him as if he was my biological father. He loves me as if I am his princess. However, I cannot help but think about my lost love. Do you ever think of me? I do not know you. I have never seen you, but I want you to know I miss you." ~ Kate

~ ~ ~

"Dear Missing Man in my Life,

I got married yesterday, and it was such a beautiful wedding. I felt beautiful on the outside; but on the inside, I cried.

I smiled through the pain, but I know life goes on. I hope I will be a good wife to my husband. All my life, I never knew how to love or to be loved by a man. I guess like always, life is going to teach me." ~ Summer

~ ~ ~

"Dear Father of Darkness,

I hope one day soon you will come to the light. My bags are heavy because I carry around tons of questions. Every day, I wonder, do I cross your path or do you cross mine? It saddens me knowing there is a possibility that we might cross paths every day, and I do not even know it. I want you to know, I am full of light and forgiveness." ~ Rachel

~ ~ ~

"Dear Human Being,

I have the right to be angry. I called you today and you told your girlfriend's son to tell me you weren't home. If you're going to lie, at least whisper further in the background. I didn't want any money, clothes or your time. I called you because I needed help. My tires were flat. You never do anything for me. The least you could do is put air in my tire. Sam's dad came by and changed my bike tube. How can you take care of Robert and not me? Did you forget I am your flesh and blood? Dad, I want you to know I am here and I am human too." ~Angry son

~ ~ ~

"Dear Mr. Full of Excuses,

Yesterday, it was the first day of school. You promised me you would send me some shoes and a couple of outfits. Three weeks passed, and I haven't received anything. I cannot wear your excuses. Your excuses cannot fit my feet. I am tired of starving because you always feed me one excuse after another. Tell the truth for once. I want you to know, you can save your excuses because I am done with all of your lies." ~ Eric

~ ~ ~

"Dear Mr. Apology,

I apologize if I am not good enough to love. I apologize if I am a burden. I apologize to my future boyfriend or husband because I do not know how to love a man. I apologize because I am bitter, hurt, and I do not know how to trust. I apologize for always being angry and in a bad mood. Momma, I apologize for blaming you for my father's absence. I do not have anyone else to blame. I cannot blame my father because I want him to love me. I apologize to myself because there are days I do not want to live because I am damaged goods. I look at myself and wonder why my father doesn't love me. Is it because I am not beautiful? Nobody tells me I am pretty. I am tired of apologizing for something I didn't do. Why do I feel like I owe you an apology? I want you to know I can love you if you allow me to." ~ Ann

~ ~ ~

"Dear Disappearing Act,

I turned seven years old today! My mother hired a magician for my birthday. I wondered why she paid someone else hundreds of dollars to "pretend" to disappear. I told my momma, she should have hired you! Disappearing Dad, you are so good at disappearing into thin air. One minute you are here and when I turn around you disappear. I want you to know, you are the greatest magician on the planet." ~ Lauren

~ ~ ~

"Dear Heart-breaker,

You are the greatest liar I've ever known. You were supposed to take me to the Father and Daughter dance. You never called or showed up. Dad, this has to stop! I am so tired of your lies. I am so tired of your broken promises. I am so tired of crying. Why do you hurt me so much? Why do you treat me this way? What have I've ever done to you? I am so tired of you always getting my hopes up just to let me down. I want you to know, that if you do not want me in your life; leave me alone." ~ Rose

~ ~ ~

"Dear Mr. You're Forgiven,

When I look at myself in the mirror, I am a reflection of you, but my actions will not copy yours. I want you to know, I graduate high school next week with honors. I never was a streetwalker. I never was on drugs. I never hung around the wrong crowd. My mother raised a fine young man, and I am ready for what the world has to offer. In a couple of months, I am going to be starting college. I am going to do great things in life. I wish you were a part of it. I want you to know, I forgive you, but I will not forget. I also want you to know, you used to hold power over my life. Life showed me it has good and bad to offer. I decided to take each day as it comes; let go of your absence and move forward. I hope all is well." ~ Marcus

~ ~ ~

"Dear Beautiful Pain,

I dust my shoulder off as I walk across the stage. I am living my best life; no thanks to you. I just earned a degree in Economic and I am about to take the world by storm and catch the wave. You know, Dad, you are every part of me; as I am of you. I set fire to yesterday. Every day, we live and learn. I want you to know, I learned a good lesson from you; and that is – if I give up and walk away, I will never have accomplished anything. Dad, I am somebody, I always have been. My wounds have healed, and I will no longer cover up the scars." ~ Brian

~ ~ ~

"Dear Coward,

I was raised by a single mother. You left me to be the man of the house. Pops, that was your job. I had no choice but to grow up at an early age. I had to run the streets to help my mom pay the bills. Because of you, my momma struggled to make pennies. The bills were overwhelming, and life tried to get the best of our family. Why couldn't you do your part? My momma had to get on welfare to keep her head above water. I hurt because my momma hurt. I was in pain because my momma was in pain. My mom worked to make sure her children had everything we needed. I want you to know you are pathetic and a sorry excuse for a man." ~ Eric

~ ~ ~

"Dear Time Expired,

I cried today because all the girls had support at their dance recital but me. I waited and waited for you to come. However, once again, you didn't live up to your word. Today, will be the last day I cry another tear, over your actions and words. I want you to know, I love you so much, but you hurt me so bad. The hurt you give can't be love; and if it is, I do not want it." ~ Ski

~ ~ ~

"Dear Mr. Give Up,

Do you honestly feel you have the right to be upset with me? I gave you chance after chance, but you were the one who let me down, over and over again. You tried to correct me as you said, "Remember, I am your father." Oh wow, did that just sink into your head after seventeen years? I know exactly who you are. You left me; your little girl who has always been in need of a father. I am only seventeen years old, and I've been in some of the worst relationships. After my boyfriend beat me so bad, I lost the sight in my left eye. I took him back because he said that he was sorry and he loved me. After he tried to beat me to death I had to run for my life. If you were in my life, I would have known the signs. I was looking for the void from not having a father. You failed me as a father. You failed me in life. I want you to know, I know exactly who you are. You are a man who gave up on his kid." ~ Clara

~ ~ ~

"Dear Point the Fingers at Me,

When are you going to own up to what you haven't done? You haven't been a father to me. You walk in and out, in and out, and think I am supposed to be okay with it. When are you going to own up to what you have done? You've done an excellent job of making my life a living hell. You taught me how to have a pity party, until one day, I was told, I have to own up and accept what I wanted, and never got as a little boy. I was told, I have to let go of what I needed as a growing boy. You point the finger at me, for your mess-up. You point the finger at me, for telling you the truth. You point the finger at me, because you walked out of my life for years. I want you to know, I am not going to have a pity party for what I needed and wanted from you in life. I want you to know, I am healing and moving on in life. I want you to hear me loud and clear, when I say, I want you to know, you are no longer welcome in my life. I have been fine without you. I am going to be better now that I know that you know exactly what I wanted you to know after all these years." ~ Emmanuel

~ ~ ~

"Dear Robbed yourself of Love,

My wife just gave birth to my son and daughter! Twins! When I held them both in my arms, I felt the kind of love that overpowers your life with joy, happiness, and letting you know you will always have a reason to live. I used to hold so much resentment against you; however, I do not anymore. I am going to love my babies to the moon and back. They are so precious, so innocent, so gentle, and the love of my life! I want you to know, I feel so sorry for you because you robbed yourself of the best feeling in the entire universe." ~ Alex

~ ~ ~

Fathers of the fatherless sons and daughters, your children do not owe you anything. The damage you caused is done; however, it doesn't mean they are damaged goods. As a Chief Guardian, it's wonderful to know our children are stronger after the storm has passed. Our children will get over and past what they expected from you. Although they received little to nothing, they know life goes on and they still exist, as the show must go on.

Fathers of the fatherless children, your sons and daughters know they are somebody – with or without you in their life.

Our children are light. They are not what has happened to them. They took their first steps without you. Before they took their first steps, the Chief Guardian has been with them every step of the way. Timing is everything, time is precious, and time doesn't wait on anyone. Fathers of the fatherless children, you are responsible for your own actions.

To the full-time fathers who are active in their son's and daughter's lives, I praise you all for giving your children so much love and the attention they need. I know you all see that life is beautiful! Your sons and daughters are truly blessed. It takes a lot of courage and dedication to embrace the leadership role of Superman! Your children know you all have their backs, through the good, bad, ups, and downs. It is a rewarding moment, for a son or daughter to know the great harmony of pure and unconditional love. It's beautiful!

My son had a doctor's appointment a couple of months ago, and for the first time ever—I saw a young father comforting his son. As he was passing his love to his child, he slept in his father's arms. I asked, "How old is your son?"

"He's fourteen months," he replied.

I smiled and said, "Please do not take offense, but I have never seen a single father at the doctor's or dentist office, etc."

He laughed, "We do not have many men who are willing to take on their responsibilities. I'm not one of them. I love my son and I refuse to let the streets, the jailhouse, or anyone else raise him, for that matter. My son turned my life around," he replied.

I smiled.

"My son saved my life. I was out there in the streets; and after my girl gave birth, I held him in my arms. When he opened his eyes, and his little fingers wrapped around my pinky, I knew right then and there my life changed," he said as he looked down at his son.

I nodded my head as I smiled.

"Life is rough without both parents. My mother raised me. I didn't have a father in my life. I am going to give my son the last of me, my all, and anything else I can give," he said as he wiped his son's face.

"He has a cold. I told my little man we are going to make him better. His mother had to work and I called off because I hate that he feels so bad. He knows daddy's going to make sure he's all better soon. It takes tender love, care, money, support, and that extra unconditional love to raise a child. I am willing to give that and more," he replied.

There are a lot of fathers of fatherless children who make the full-time fathers, who are very involved in their children's lives, look bad. I know there are good fathers out there because my father is one of them. My children's Grandpa Chris is an amazing grandpa as well. Since my children were in kindergarten, he never missed Grandparent's Day, he never missed a birthday party or sports event, and he always makes time for his grandchildren. He takes them to the movies, park, etc. He taught my oldest son how to drive and took him to get his driver's licenses—the smallest things such as spending time counts the most. They are memories that will always be remembered. Grandpa Chris is an amazing grandpa! He is truly appreciated!

Fathers who are in their children's lives, continue to help your sons and daughters move mountains. You all are your children's security blankets. You all are your son's and daughter's joy in life. As you nurture your children, they will flourish. Thank you! Congratulations on a job well done!

Fathers of the fatherless sons and daughters, you all need to get on the full-time ship of love, support, and financial help. Your parental alienation is emotional child abuse. As you violate fatherhood, your children build up walls and it is not so easy for them to forgive. If it's not too late, you need to make it right.

Fathers of the fatherless sons and daughters, we all make mistakes and we always will. However, not being a part of your children's lives isn't a mistake; it's a choice. When all's said and done, the ship is always pressing forward. At the beginning and end of the day, you all only have yourselves to blame.

10

To Daddy with Love

Daddy, I always get emotional when I talk about you because you've always been my first love. By you being in my life you have given me great strength of determination. I thank you for always telling me to go for what I believe in. You always say, "Baby girl, you got everything you need; you have to figure out how to use what you have." There were days when I wanted to give up, but giving up was never an option. Crying on your shoulder gave me comfort, mixed with the strength to take off and fly.

Daddy, your unconditional love chased away my fears. Your protection and security gave me the courage to charge and take flight as I went into the unknown and I came out as a warrior.

Daddy, I cannot thank you enough for your time. Your time meant and means the world to me. Your time makes every day special. Your time makes me a powerhouse. Your time opens many doors of possibilities. Your time taught me I have the right to be wrong; and that my mistakes will make me strong, as they are lessons learned.

As a little girl, Daddy, I admired your determination, courage, and strength.

Thank you, Daddy, for leading by example and for letting me know that I have a mind of my own, and the only approval that matters is mine. Life has a funny way of testing what I was taught, but as you always reminded me; everyone's opinion is just that; an opinion. As you would say, "Lena, what do you think?"

Your questions were simple but meaningful. It made me think long and hard about my life. Daddy, because of your love I dared to be different as I walked my own path of tall grass while other people took the easy path where the grass was always cut. Daddy, because of your support and encouraging words, I walked the path of high grass, and as I walked down the path, I cut the grass along the way. It wasn't easy; as a matter of fact, it was very challenging. However, what matters and counts the most is that I do not have to walk the path alone—because I know for a fact, that you will always have my back and that you will be with me every step of the way.

Daddy, you always kept it real, and I love you so much for always being honest. When I was in the wrong, you were very strict with your rules and regulations, but your rules and regulations made me the strong woman I am today.

When I was at my lowest point you were always there for me; you always made time to listen to my many problems. When I felt like the world had turned its back against me; Daddy, you were always there; and I cannot say thank you enough. Through the rough times and all the chaos, you were always there to lend a helping hand, an ear, and/or your presence.

Daddy, I know it wasn't easy raising three little girls. Boy oh boy, thanks to you, Daddy, we had mouths on us. You always told your girls to never, ever, be afraid to speak our truth. There were times in school when we would speak our minds, and nearly every day, you were getting phone calls from our teachers. After you talked to our teachers you would ask us what happened. We would say, "Well, Daddy, you said we should always speak our truth." It wasn't funny then, but it *is* funny now because I can only imagine what you went through with three little girls.

Daddy, you are the best daddy in the entire universe. Every weekend, we would head to the country and ride our horses, Frisco and Savannah. You always made sure we were saddled up as you led us on the trail. Your time with your girls was priceless!

Thank you so much, Daddy, for making so many sacrifices for your girls. When everyone judged us, you always had our backs. You made sure your girls were taken care of mentally, spiritually, and emotionally. Thank you,

Daddy.

Every Wednesday night, you would play the organ as my sisters and I would sing, *My God is Real*. We would sing for hours as Momma fixed dinner.

Our science projects were the best! You would come home with so much work to do. As your drawing board was laid out with the blueprints lying across it, my sisters and I would run in your office and ask for help with our science projects or math homework. The best science project ever was when you used Pogo Balls and turned them into all of the planets in the universe. We got First Place!

When my sisters and I needed help with our math homework; that was the best! We thought we were rich when you used money and coins to help us solve problems. To top it off, you let us keep all the money we used. Daddy, thank you for helping us with our projects, homework, and for giving us your time. You made homework fun!

Daddy, I remember when we were at Service Merchandise and I saw a computer that I loved. I said, "Look, Daddy, look, isn't this cool?" You said, "Yes. It is. Put it back."

I cried because I didn't get the Computer 1000.

The following week, you came home and asked me to get your suitcase out of the car and bring in the black bag from the front seat. As I did as I was asked. You said, "Oh, take the box out of the bag for me." I took the box out of the bag – and it was a Computer 1000!

"A Computer 1000!" I screamed joyfully.

I ran into your arms as you asked, "Did you think I was going to let my baby girl cry?"

"Daddy, you did let me cry. I cried all the way home too," I replied.

Daddy, you laughed as you kissed me on the cheek and said, "I won't ever put a tear in my baby girl's eyes again."

Daddy, you are truly appreciated. You never made your girls feel anything less than your princesses. When I look back it is so precious how you were so patient with us. Everyone was so scared of you because you were so direct, cutthroat, and never sugar-coated anything. However, Daddy, you were and still are so gentle with your girls.

Daddy, you cannot ever be replaced! You raised three beautiful, smart, outgoing, and "speak our truth" young girls who are now women. Daddy, there isn't a man alive that could ever take your place. Daddy, your love is never-ending and you are one-of-a-kind!

Thank you, daddy for your unconditional love. Daddy, you are my first love, you are my joy, you are my happiness, and I am truly blessed. I love you so much, Daddy, and always remember, you will always be the man of my life.

Love always,

Your Baby Girl, Lena

Introduction for the book:
A Woman's Love is Never Good Enough 2nd edition

Love.

What is love? It is the essence of the unknown and will overwhelm you if you do not realize you are giving too much of yourself.

Love is an intense emotion that will take a toll on you mentally, emotionally, and physically in an unselfish, yet bittersweet way that develops into a deep affection; and sometimes, an unknown outcome.

Love is filled with a lot of sacrifices and resentment and is underestimated in so many ways. It is something of a Catch-22 and an overwhelming source of empowerment. You might feel as though love didn't give you an answer to the questions that you asked. You've been waiting for days, even years; and perhaps you will never receive an answer at all. Maybe you've received an answer; however, it wasn't what you expected. The question is—did you accept the answer, or are you still searching for the answer you desire?

Love is a strange word. It can be misleading and confusing. It can break you down with tender grace and mercy, while at the same time building you up to become a powerful force—and after that, you will never be the same.

The ripple effects of love are beautiful and peaceful, yet can also be disturbing and ruthless. At times, love takes advantage of its powers; it causes you to suffer from loving someone too much and finding yourself lost, without hope and giving too much of yourself to the point that you suffer because you're neglecting yourself. It can cause you to lose faith. Its tremendous effect has a full impact as you find peace and happiness in your life.

Love will open your eyes to realize you are not the victim; instead, you are victorious over the trials, battles, and challenges of life.

Love will show you that you do not have to search for it because it abides in you whole-heartedly. Love can be bittersweet but its grace is patience. Love is difficult but its mercy is tender. At times love might make you feel empty but you are never alone.

Love abounds against all odds. One thing about love is that it comes with many sacrifices. Its good intentions always reassure you that in order to love someone else, you must be willing to love yourself first.

Introduction for the book:
I'm Speaking Up but Your Not Listening 2nd edition

We want to protect our children by any means necessary. Sadly, we cannot be with them every moment of the day. I never thought I would have to teach my children to defend themselves at such a young age. Children are supposed to be free spirits, dream chasers, and thinking of limitless opportunities. They are supposed to be filled with light that shines with happiness and joy that shouldn't be dimmed or filled with darkness and fear.

Children should be living carefree lives and always smiling, laughing, filled with peace, and harmony; not worrying about the troubles of what tomorrow may bring. Our children should have a wide range of imagination and think about the greatest achievements that they want to accomplish; not making sacrifices by having to give up their clothes, lunch money, or being robbed of their personality, and stripped of their self-esteem.

As parents, guardians, teachers, and school administrators, we should be giving our children better days, we are the outcome of their future, we are the pieces of the puzzle – pieces that restore their shattered confidence. When our children are hopeless, we are the light that shines brightly to renew their hope. Our love and actions are the hope that floats to restore what was lost and to renew strength that they never imagined existed.

We are our children's voices when all else has failed. As parents, guardians, teachers, and school administrators, we have to be more involved in our children's lives. Bullying shouldn't be taken lightly. However, it's a sad fact that bullying is played down in schools by some teachers, administrators, and sometimes at home by the parents.

We have to change this continuous cycle. It has gone on too far for way too long. Our children shouldn't be victims of suicide or have suicidal thoughts because someone thinks they have the ability to strip them bit by bit and piece by piece of their birthright of life.

We must fight for our children; our voices are louder and the roar of our demand for change will be heard loud and clear. We will burn the ashes of fear from our children because we are a source of empowerment.

Our children are special, they are unique, they are a gift, and they are our children that we love dearly. Without a doubt, change will come and we must make that change happen because bullying is not accepted.

We shouldn't give anyone the ability to rob our children of happiness. We have the power to change the situation. For those who feel as though bullying is an unknown situation, let's dare to be different and make the situation known by opening the problem at hand by speaking up and finding a solution to the problem. We should always remember, when a problem occurs, we must not forget that there's always a solution.

Now is the time to decide to make the change. Now is the time to dissect and look at every angle in the distasteful world of bullying. Now is the time for us to put our best foot forward and take on the responsibility of saving our children from being killed or destroyed by bullying; also, known as the Silent Killer. Our children shouldn't be prisoners of what a bully has cast on them. Our children want their voices to be heard; and as the adults in charge, our voices deserve to be heard.

The time has come to take action to stop bullying – and the time is now!

Introduction for the book:
No Cross, No Crown: Trust God Through the Battle 2nd edition

"For I know the plans I have for you," declares the LORD, "Plans to prosper you and not to harm you, plans to give you hope and a future" (Jeremiah 29:11).

Life is full of surprises. We find ourselves free-falling as we love freely; rejoicing in giving and not looking for anything in return; smiling without expecting to grieve; laughing not knowing pain is right around the corner. When clouds begin to block the sunlight and the storm is on the way, we move toward shelter because we know that when it rains, it pours. When rain destroys the life we have built, it is hard for some of us to start over. We may think to start over is a bad thing; however, we never take time out to have a clear understanding of why the rain took its course. We begin to think the worst of a bad situation because the thunder shook our confidence, the lightning struck our fears into action, the rain flooded our happiness, and the clouds clouded our train of thought to the point we cannot think clearly.

Sometimes we find ourselves headed down a one-way street; sooner or later we have to make a decision to turn left or right. We need to take the right steps, and use the advantage of the clouds so we can see clearly because the sun can be too bright and hinder our ability to see. That is when we have to step back, reevaluate our life, and understand the meaning of No Cross No Crown.

ABOUT THE AUTHOR

Charlena E. Jackson, B.S., M.S., M.H.A. is a professor at a university in Georgia. She is a prolific writer and has published several books, among them being: No Cross, No Crown: Trust God Through the Battle (1st & 2nd edition), Teachers Just Don't Understand Bullying Hurts (1st & 2nd edition), I'm Speaking Up but You're Not Listening (1st & 2nd edition), A Woman's Love is Never Good Enough (1st & 2nd edition), Dear Fathers of the Fatherless Children, Dying on the Inside and Suffocating on the Outside, and Unapologetic for My Flaws and All (1st and 2nd edition). Her positive, dedicated, and determined attitude has encouraged many people to put up a good fight for justice and to be treated with respect. She is currently working on her Ph.D. in Healthcare Administration. Charlena is a much-loved inspirational speaker. She loves to read, roller skate, cycle, write, and travel. Charlenaejackson@gmail.com